The Police and Me

The Police and Me

As The Thin Blue Line Got Thinner

John Sharpe

HAYLOFT PUBLISHING LTD

First published by Hayloft Publishing Ltd., 2017

© John Sharpe, 2017

The right of John Sharpe to be identified as the Author of the Work has been asserted by him in accordance with the Copyright, Designs and Patents Act 1988

All rights reserved. Apart from any use permitted under UK copyright law no part of this publication may be reproduced, stored in a retrieval system, or transmitted, in any form or by any means without the prior written permission of the publisher, nor be otherwise circulated in any form of binding or cover other than that in which it is published and without a similar condition being imposed on the subsequent purchaser.

A CIP catalogue record for this book is available from the British Library

ISBN 978-1-910237-31-1

Printed by Bell & Bain Ltd., Scotland.

Hayloft policy is to use papers that are natural, renewable and recyclable products and made from wood grown in sustainable forests. The logging and manufacturing processes are expected to conform to the environmental regulations of the country of origin.

Hayloft Publishing Ltd,
a company registered in England number 4802586
2 Staveley Mill Yard, Staveley, Kendal, LA8 9LR (registered office)
L'Ancien Presbytère, 21460 Corsaint, France (editorial office)

Email: books@hayloft.eu
Tel: 07971 352473
www.hayloft.eu

Frontispiece: *Policeman and dog in a blizzard, Penrith, 1960s*

*The policeman stands for good citizenship;
he is a reality that the most ignorant can comprehend*
From a 1960s police text book, quoting an earlier authority

Also by John Sharpe

COLOURFUL CHARACTERS OF CUMBRIA'S EDEN VALLEY
ISBN 978-1-910237-08-3

JOHN METCALFE CARLETON: GEORGIAN RAKE OF THE EDEN VALLEY

THE WORKMAN BROTHERS:
ENGLISH PIONEERS OF THE AMERICAN WEST
(shortlisted for the 2014 Lake District Book of the Year Award)

Available to buy or order at any local bookshop

CONTENTS

Preface		ix
Foreword		x
1	Introduction:	1
	Job interview at Police HQ; Police Training Centre at Warrington	
2	First Posting:	11
	Foot patrol; colourful colleagues; first arrests; 'the blue light', 'Kendal Mary' and other local characters; road accidents; sudden deaths; 'domestics'; murder of a policeman and the search for a gunman	
3	Headquarters Traffic Patrol:	38
	Motorcycle patrol; road accidents; arrests for drink driving (before the breathalyser); vehicle theft and attempted murder; M6 motorway construction	
4	Staff Officer:	72
	An 'old style' Chief Constable and his minions; police discipline procedure; promotion system in theory and practice, Bramshill Police College	
5	The Sub-Division:	106
	Probationer problems; police role in local courts; colourful magistrates' clerks; deaths on roads, lakes and fells; Freemasonry in the police	
6	Project Team:	138
	A leap in the dark; computer system and reflections on police management; The Miners' Strike; major new PACE Act planning; a month in Scarborough	
7	Complaints and Discipline:	171
	'Who will watch the watchers themselves?' law and the system in practice; conciliation or investigation? some bizarre allegations; prison encounters	
About the Author		208

PREFACE

John Sharpe's *The Police and Me*, an extended memoir of his distinguished career in the Cumbria Police Force, is the latest instalment in a remarkable series of his fine publications in Cumbrian history, including the recent *Colourful Characters of Cumbria's Eden Valley*. Indeed, 'characters' are John Sharpe's forté – and the reason why he is in such demand on the local history lecture circuit. John has an enviable ability to capture a personality, with unforgettable vignettes like that of lady of the night (or 'diesel queen') Kendal Mary, who provided home comforts for lonely A6 truckers. But John's approach to humanity in all its infinite variety is also the key to his attitude to policing – little of theory but everything of common sense, with broad sympathy and a degree of tolerance of frailty founded in experience and practical wisdom.

    Finely written in highly readable English and in the style of a good-humoured and often hilarious fireside chat, Sharpe's career autobiography has a serious side as well. Not only does *The Police and Me* make a substantial contribution to modern Cumbrian social history but it offers profoundly considered judgements on what British policing at its best ought to be: the bobby as a tribune of the community.

Michael Mullett
Emeritus Professor of Cultural and Religious History
University of Lancaster
20 vii 16

FOREWORD

John Sharpe lives at Clifton near Penrith on the eastern fringe of the English Lake District. A Cumbrian whose forebears through several generations were masons and builders in a modest way of business in the west of the county, he broke the ancestral thread by going to university in the 1950s and doing his National Service in the Army before working for a short time in a bank and at the British Nuclear Fuels factory at Sellafield.

He joined the police in 1963. His reasons for that had something to do with vague notions of public service together with a desire for a bit of variety and maybe even some excitement. Being unimpressed by what he had seen of trade union activities, he may also have been motivated to some extent by the knowledge that the police did not have a union (although subsequent experience sometimes led him to think it was a job where a union was particularly needed).

Some of us will remember 1963 better than others, but it was an eventful year. It was the year of the Great Train Robbery and the assassination of President Kennedy. The first James Bond film hit the cinema screens and the Beatles recorded their first LP, while we were just getting used to the drama of working-class life on Manchester's *Coronation Street*. In politics, Harold Wilson became Labour leader on the death of Hugh Gaitskell, and the Profumo affair convulsed the press and rocked the establishment. Currency was our age-old pounds, shillings and pence, and strictly black and white television showed images of near traffic-free streets with hardly a foreign-made car to be seen.

Policing methods in 1963 were little changed from what

they had been in Victorian times. Most policemen – and there were very few policewomen – still went about on their feet. There were no Police Community Support Officers, traffic wardens, personal radios, tasers or computers and precious few vehicles. *Dixon of Dock Green* represented the typical policeman for many people, it seemed, and TV's controversial new *Z-Cars* had only just started to challenge that cosy image.

The police force (it was not fashionable to call it a service in 1963) was a mysterious organisation then – and probably still is, despite all the interest in it that manifests itself in the press and on television, both fact and fiction. The author saw all sorts of organisational changes from the inside before leaving the job in 1992. This, then, is one individual's attempt to answer the question: 'What was it like to do nearly 30 years in a county police force at a time of rapid change?'

Some previous efforts to describe life in the police have tended to focus on accounts of the kind of funny (in both senses) incidents that fall to the lot of the uniformed constable. What follows here includes an element of that approach (without presuming to mount a challenge to what has appeared before), but it is much more of an autobiographical outline of the experiences of someone who had the good fortune to serve in quite a number of totally different capacities within the job. A lot of the book is concerned with police organisation and management, with ordinary people 'drest in a little brief authority.' This is the unseen aspect of policing – and it may be no less interesting for that.

The book was drafted initially around 1990, at a time of apparently mounting criticism of police performance in general and of management in particular. Other writing challenges then got in the author's way, and over two decades elapsed before his pen found policing again as a once-familiar service disappeared from the streets amid seemingly worsening press publicity and massive budget cuts. He would argue that the resulting delay does nothing to render his account irrelevant; indeed, that twenty-odd years maturing in the cask may even have enriched the product.

Insofar as this book has a serious side, its secondary objective is to be a modest contribution to the continuing debate about the role of the police; and in that sense it sets out to be analytical and critical where appropriate but also constructive and fair. The tone, however, is intended to be essentially humorous without being frivolous, although what degree of success attends that basic aim will be a matter of opinion. If a cynical element creeps in at times then the proffered excuse is that that is hardly surprising after 29 years in a job that sometimes seemed driven by cynicism. But this is not a rosy story of police life: things are less than perfect, and it is a view of the service from the inside, warts and all.

The book is based on original material as well as a good memory for detail, and is entirely factual. Names are used sparingly, and are avoided if they seem likely to cause embarrassment.

1
INTRODUCTION

It was a cold December morning in 1962 when I reported for interview at the imposing Georgian manor house that was now Police Headquarters. At the age of 25, with experience behind me ranging from the academic life to National Service in the Army, I thought I must have at least some of the basic qualifications a policeman needed. Perhaps I was a bit over-optimistic because I hardly contemplated the probable consequences of failure – a return to the confines of an office job behind a factory fence.

I was shown into a large first floor office where a uniformed inspector was seated at a desk with six empty chairs facing him on the other side of the room. I took one of the chairs and sat in silence. The inspector kept his head down over his desk. I was obviously first of the day's hopefuls to arrive, but over the next few minutes or so four more young men were ushered into the office and sat down. The inspector took no notice of us, and we were all too nervous to speak. You could have heard a pin drop.

Suddenly, after a slight lull when I began to think chair number six was not going to be taken, the last applicant arrived. He was a tall young man with a moustache and a military bearing, as they used to say. Unlike the rest of us, he was complete with brief-case and papers that he proceeded to flourish, while even going so far as to engage the attention of the taciturn inspector opposite us. I was impressed, well nearly, but for my above-mentioned bit of experience in the Army, where such exhibitionism would have been dismissed as bull.

Eventually, and with relief, we all stood up to be led

elsewhere in the building. The administration inspector found his voice at last to pass some remark about me being the shortest of the bunch (at 5'9' and a bit).

My turn came to be interviewed by the chief constable. No nonsense then with recruiting panels; it was the top man and nobody else. I had been advised by the village constable back home to address the chief as 'Sir' at every opportunity. No problem there – my Army experience stood me in good stead on that one. I also remembered various smart phrases like 'Keeping a finger on the public pulse' that another policeman friend had told me might go down well. That of course gave the chief an opportunity to outsmart me by remarking that in dealing with members of the public a policeman sometimes had to get hold of more than their pulse.

After the chief's interview the next trip was into town to see the police surgeon, with the dire warning ringing in our ears from an admin constable that 'You might have got past the Chief, but wait 'til you see Dr Mel!' The elderly doctor's examination went much as would be expected until he came to the colour test, which I failed. It consisted of a series of cards with a lot of coloured dots on them. The dots were not all the same colour, but some were, and it should have been possible to see a colour pattern on each card that produced a single figure, e.g. a figure five in pink dots on a card that otherwise contained mainly red dots. I had had mixed success with this test before, so I was not unduly surprised by the result. 'Dr. Mel' didn't seem bothered. He just pointed at pens and things on his desk and asked what colour each was. I must have given the right answers because he passed me without further ado.

Then the candidates who had satisfied both the chief and the doctor were wheeled back into the former's office. There were just two of us – myself and the flamboyant young man who had taken the inspector's office by storm earlier that morning. The chief constable told us he was appointing us both. He went on to give us a little pep-talk about our apparent academic ability and Army experience and so on and went on to say he would be expecting quite a lot from us. He told us he had two members of the force on the first Special Course at the Police College at Bramshill in Hampshire, who had qualified for the course by reason of outstanding success in the sergeants' promotion exam. The pair were on the one-year accelerated promotion course as temporary sergeants with just five years' police service, and successful completion of the course would mean that their ranks would be made substantive. There were only 20 from the whole country on this first Special Course, and the chief constable was clearly quite proud that his relatively small force had produced two of them.

My new found friend and I were quite elated, naturally. I returned home in good spirits, looking forward to what I was sure would be quite an adventure.

I had been attracted to the idea of joining the police for some time and my resolve to apply for the job had been strengthened by increasing disillusionment with the prospect of continuing office work. Perhaps also, on reflection, I had got more accustomed than I thought at the time to the attractions of a uniformed life as a rather reluctant national serviceman and imagined that the police service might have some similarities with the Army, whose drawbacks by then were beginning to fade from memory. My actual knowledge of the police was not very great. Indeed, it was as mysterious an organisation to me as it would be to many people, but perhaps that was part of the attraction. Maybe also I had been lucky because my previous encounters with policemen had been few and far between, and they had always left me with impressions that were entirely favourable.

My first brush with the law was when I was about thirteen

years of age and was casually pedalling my bike without my hands on the handlebars. I thought the village policeman who spotted the misdemeanour and spoke to me about it was maybe a bit officious, but in my efforts to think of an excuse I said something that might have seemed a bit on the clever side so perhaps he was right to be slightly annoyed.

Subsequent offences on my part remained undetected until 13 July 1960. Bastille Day on 14 July is one of the dates I can always guarantee to remember because that day in 1960 was my last day in the khaki uniform. The night before was the occasion of a demob celebration for about eight of us national servicemen, and a coach-load of us and our Army colleagues went by coach to a Buckinghamshire country pub for the evening.

A pleasant evening of conviviality and reminiscing ended for some reason with a mini-riot involving two factions led by the Cockneys and the Geordies among us. A lone village policeman appeared as if by magic and bundled everyone onto the bus very efficiently, to get the trouble mobile and away off his patch. It was very nicely done – no shouting, no fuss, no sending for back-up and no arrests for breach of the peace or whatever.

About a year later I was riding a motorcycle through a Lancashire town when a police car 'appeared from nowhere' to sweep in front of me and pull me up for exceeding the 30 mph speed limit. When I got stopped at the roadside, I was surprised to find that two or three other motorcyclists had also stopped behind me. With the restricted rear view from a motorcycle, I had been unaware of their presence until then (and that of course applied to the police car as well). Anyway, the policeman told us the speed he had recorded in following us and sent us on our way. The road was deserted at the time, our speed, though illegal, had not been outrageous and he used his discretion. (Maybe also he was nearing his finishing time and thought he hadn't time to make out all the offence reports).

Not long before I joined the police I was driving in a Cumbrian town that was quite well-known to me, and in a moment's inattention I found myself travelling the wrong way along a one-way street. I had not gone far when realisation dawned, and simultaneously a young policeman appeared and stopped me. No harm had been done, and again the situation was dealt with courteously and without overreaction or brandishing notebook and pen.

These encounters were all quite trivial but nevertheless significant in their own way. I suppose I had had no particular reason to mistrust the police and none of these incidents did anything to alter my overall impression of the organisation. All the individuals concerned were courteous and did not say or do any more than they had to. It occurred to me later on that the way these issues were dealt with probably had something to do with the formulation of an idea that a reasonable guiding principle of policing might be to do the minimum necessary to secure the objective. Symptomatic of idealism, no doubt, but more of that later.

It was 11 January 1963 when I reported back to police headquarters to be kitted out and sworn in. This time I was committed and it was for real. I found there were six of us starting in the job that day. Three were young ex-police cadets who were now being appointed to the regular force and the three others included of course myself and my assertive friend from the day of the interview the previous month.

One of my most vivid recollections of this momentous day was of standing in the force stores for issue of uniform and accoutrements by the formidable Ernie, storeman extraordinary. As every good storeman doubtless should, he issued every item of clothing and equipment – staff (truncheon), handcuffs and whistle – with an air of reluctance that might have suggested he was paying for it out of his own pocket. And you had to fit his gear rather than the other way round.

It occurred to me later that of the six who reported to the stores that day I was the only one who remained a member of the police force locally. Three left the job altogether and two transferred elsewhere. We got our Warrant Cards and were taken down to the local Magistrates' Court to be sworn in before the Justices. Back at HQ we were involved in final documentation and signing for membership of various bodies like the Police Federation and the Widows and Orphans Fund, filling in forms for things that I for one did not really understand the significance of but did not see fit to query.

It was a Sunday afternoon when we got on the train for the 100-mile trip south to the regional police training centre at Bruche near Warrington in Lancashire. As the journey progressed, the winter fog got thicker, the train slowed down and eventually we noticed we were travelling through Manchester. It turned out that the train had been diverted because of the weather, and eventually we finished up at Crewe in Cheshire, some 20 miles past our intended destination in Warrington. And it was really foggy. An inauspicious start to a police career!

By now of course it was well past the time when we should have been at Warrington. Whether or not anyone at the training centre was really worried about us Cumbrians, it was obviously courteous to try and let them know where we were. Here again, our assertive friend came to the fore as spokesman for the hapless band of weary travellers and managed to get through on the 'phone to Bruche. We got there eventually, about six hours late, after a two-hour journey that had actually taken eight.

INTRODUCTION

Unlike the rest of the 100-odd recruits from the North West police forces who were beginning the same three-month initial training course, we representatives of the most far-flung outpost of the region did not have the advantage of the few hours' acclimatisation on the Sunday evening. Sitting in the dining hall at breakfast next morning, feeling slightly unready for all this activity, I looked round the assembled throng of uniformed figures and focused particularly on a strutting sergeant with a slashed cap peak and an air of the Guards about him. Obviously he was the drill sergeant and officer-in-charge of breakfast arrangements that day. It occurred to me that I had emerged from a similar environment not all that long before, and I wondered for a moment if I had done the right thing after all.

However, I consoled myself with the thought that a police training centre could hardly be as tough as Aldershot had been in 1958, and assuming I survived the course I was going back to my home county. In any case, we were obviously going to be quite busy, without too much time for idle reflection. There was no going back now.

This training centre near Warrington was about the largest in the country. Serving the whole North West Region, it catered for the initial police training needs of the counties of Cumberland, Westmorland, Lancashire, Cheshire and the Isle of Man, along with all the city and borough police forces in the area, such as Manchester and Liverpool.

This was before the major police re-organisation of the later 1960s when many forces amalgamated; and in 1963 there was a surprising number of separate forces. Some, like Carlisle City Police, Barrow Borough and Bootle Borough had a total strength of only about 100, but each had its own identity with its own Chief Constable and police authority. The variety was most noticeable at Bruche, with a multiplicity of helmet badges and even differences in appearance of the various uniforms.

There was a new intake of recruits at the training centre every month, with about 100 coming in at a time, so there were around 300 on the initial course. Bruche also did a continuation course of a couple of weeks for probationers at the one-year stage, so there must have been a total of around 400 students there at any one time. Each class of 20 or so was in the charge of a sergeant and the place had a few higher ranks on the instructional staff as well. All the instructors were on secondment from the various forces in the Northern Region.

The police 'bible' at the time was Moriarty's *Police Law*, which you were advised to acquire but had to buy yourself. Recruits were issued with a copy of the Student Lesson Notes, which formed the basis of the initial course at all regional police training centres. Most of the time at Bruche would be taken up with formal instruction in a class-room environment. None of your discussion groups or 'facilitative learning' then, although of course you could ask questions in class, and individuals would get questions suddenly thrown at them to check if they were awake. There was also a fair bit of physical activity like drill (easy for me with the Army fresh in my mind) and swimming (difficult). First Aid was bit of a bore, I'm afraid.

The first phase of the course concentrated logically enough on police history, with particular emphasis on significant milestones like the creation of the Metropolitan Police in 1829, the County and Borough Police Act 1856 (making compulsory the formation of a police force in every borough and county), the Desborough Committee of 1919 leading to standardisation of police pay and conditions, and the Oaksey Committee of 1948. More recently, various well publicised police problems in the late 1950s had led to the 1960 Royal Commission ('Willink'), which had just issued its interim report recommending a substantial increase in pay. As a matter of interest, my first month's net pay – not a full month because I had started on the 11th – was £26/7/1 (£26.35p). The first full month was February 1963 at £41/9/3 (£41.45p). Gross pay was £535 per annum at this time.

The initial training course also dealt with police organisation and ranks, and divided up the rudiments of the law into three broad headings under Crime, Traffic and General Police Duties. All kinds of quaint terms were banded about then, like references to 'rogues and vagabonds' and 'incorrigible rogues' under the Vagrancy Act 1824, the 'Four Night Misdemeanours' under the same Act (I think) and the Town Police Clauses Act's prohibition on nuisances like beating doormats in the street after 8am (or was it before 8am?)

Practical incidents also were set up like road traffic accidents (RTAs in police jargon), dealing with drunks and protecting the scene of a crime, but one thread that seemed to run through the whole course was the learning by heart of Definitions. If I remember rightly, there were 83 of them, beginning with the definition of Constable, and including quite complicated ones like that of a Pedlar and a Hawker. The definition of Larceny was a real tester, covering all aspects of the offence and running to about a page and a half. There was no alternative to sitting down regularly with your list of definitions and learning them parrot-fashion.

Recruits at the training centre came from a fair cross-section of backgrounds, although most would no doubt have accepted that they did not 'come from the class of gentlemen', as the old Victorian specification for the job so nicely put it. Some like me had been in the armed forces but most no doubt had just wanted an early change from being butchers, bakers and candlestick makers. An appreciable proportion at this time were ex-cadets who had already been associated with the police for two or three years in most cases. They of course were the knowledgable ones who had an advantage over the rest of us in being able to bandy about mysterious terms like 'HORT/1', 'RTA', 'D&D': and 'Section 47'.[1]

The cadets in general, though, left me rather uneasy, because at the age of nineteen they had had no working life outside the confines of the police service. I tended to sympathise with the view of the 1949 Oaksey Report which turned out to have said: 'Our main objection to any considerable expansion of the cadet system is that policemen have to deal with people in all walks of life and should have had as much experience as possible of men and manners outside the orbit of the police service.' Despite encountering one or two notable exceptions, my early misgivings about the cadet system were not dispelled by subsequent experience. More on this point later.

My time at the training centre ended in April 1963 and I was posted to the town of Kendal. The training centre had been a worthwhile experience but I was looking forward to the job for real. I knew a bit about the theory but virtually nothing about the context.

---

1 HORT/1 – Form to produce driving doouments.
  RTA – Road traffic accident
  D&D – Drunk and disorderly
  Section 47 – Actual bodily harm (sec 47, Offences against the Person Act).

2
FIRST POSTING

After a couple of days back at police headquarters on what was rather euphemistically called a local procedure course, I arrived in Kendal, the administrative centre of the old county of Westmorland (though not the county town, which honour for historical reasons still went to the much smaller Appleby, about 25 miles away).

Kendal was a town of about 20,000 people that owed its origins mainly to the wool trade (Motto – *Pannus Mini Panis*, or Wool is my Bread, for the non-Latin scholars). Sitting astride the main north-south A6 road, it was a busy town that was sometimes referred to as the Gateway to the Lakes. But being quite unfamiliar with the area, what particularly struck me right away was the town's range of industry and business activity. Apart from being the home of K Shoes and the headquarters of Provincial Insurance (reputedly the only such HQ outside London), Kendal made mint cake (obviously), snuff, water turbines, carpets, socks and paper, to name but a few. Unemployment was virtually nil and could only have consisted of the unemployable.

Until as late as 1947, Kendal Borough had its own police force with a chief constable and a chief inspector as his deputy. Several of the town police staff in 1963 had joined the old borough force before it was taken over by the county. In 1963 there was a fairly new police station that was the headquarters of the division covering the whole of the county of Westmorland. Divisional police strength was about 100, of whom around a third were based at Kendal. The man in charge was the superintendent, and there were two uniformed inspectors and about half a dozen sergeants, while the rest of course were constables, including one policewoman.

An early introduction was to the superintendent, to be given the necessary pep-talk about standards required. The super was a plumply avuncular man in his 50s who had joined the police around 1930. In my case he was particularly interested that I came from Seascale in West Cumberland. He did tell me that he had been stationed at Seascale as the village bobby in 1934 when he lodged with a now elderly lady of our mutual acquaintance. He went on to say that he was a very zealous young officer in those days who was always on the look-out for interesting cases to report. However, Seascale then was a very respectable place, and despite all his best efforts at crime detection the only case he ever had was a horse and cart without lights. (Actually, that incident must have stuck in his mind because he told me the same story several times subsequently, the last time about 25 years after the first and long after he had retired from the force).

The two inspectors were something of a contrasting pair. One was a notably courteous and correct sort of man whose training and administrative inclinations were apt to manifest themselves in his habit of meeting probationers like myself on the street and trying to catch them out with a sudden demand for a legal definition or whatever. On the other hand, 'Foxy', as the other inspector was called behind his back (affectionately, no doubt), was a blunt spoken individual with markedly less concern for social niceties than his colleague. The same man also had a nasty habit of singling young policemen out for a reprimand at parade times, which was a bit embarrassing for the individual concerned, but in general he was fair and his bark was worse than his bite, as they say.

One sergeant whose path often crossed mine at this time

was something of a humorist who was quite tickled that I not only knew the meaning of the Latin town motto but could also translate the pretentious inscription over the entrance to the local gas works *Ex Fumo Dare Lucem* ('To give light from smoke', for anyone who is interested but does not have fourth-form Latin). I had felt sure all along that a bit of Latin was bound to be of use in the police force… This man's colleague, sergeant number two, also had a sense of humour but unfortunately was inclined to criticise people behind their backs so he needed to be treated with caution.

The third sergeant was a middle-aged man who had been promoted with about 25 years' service, which was unusual even in a fairly small rural force like Cumbria. Paperwork was a chore for him and arrests unnecessary. I remember standing with him in the town centre late one night when a man rushed out of the Town Hall where there was a dance in progress. He ran over to us and gasped, 'There's all hell let loose in there!' Always keen to deal with such things in his own way, Big Jim just said to me, 'Hang on here a minute' and walked off at a measured pace across the road into the Town Hall. Nothing happened for a couple of minutes. Then the Town Hall's swing doors burst open and Big Jim emerged on to the street, propelling two youths, one with each hand by the back of the neck. That was the end of it – no arrests for breach of the peace or drunk and disorderly or whatever, and probably no more trouble in the dance that night either.

Sergeant number four was a very sound sort of man in my view. He did not do more than was strictly necessary in any given set of circumstances but he was a lot more orthodox in his approach than the aforementioned old-style sergeant. An ex-naval man if I remember rightly, he had a keen sense of humour and always seemed very calm and collected, with a courteous manner towards the public. He was also patient and tolerant with new starters like myself. All in all, I thought he came over as a practical policeman who was a particularly good example to probationers in his charge.

Not long after I was posted to Kendal, we were joined by a fifth sergeant. His qualities of maturity and common sense fell markedly below the standards set by the other four sergeants, although in fairness I suppose he was quite a bit younger than they were both in years and in length of police service. But I thought any policeman worth the name would hardly want to hide behind trees in the town park to report children breaching the bye-laws by riding their bikes on the footpaths, or lurk in the darkness up alleyways outside fish and chip shops to catch people dropping litter. And he was of the two men from our force on the first Police College Special Course that the chief constable had held out as an example to the two of us whom he had appointed that day in January!

In fairness to the Special Course concept, the rules were changed for entry to subsequent such courses to include qualification by interview as well as by examination results. However, a good exam result alone had got our hero on the first rung of the promotion ladder at an early stage, and I can reveal that his rise to stardom did not end there, although he did take his talents elsewhere in the country to achieve the next higher rank.

So the sergeants and the higher ranks at my first station were not a bad lot, and I for one soon found myself at home and quite comfortable in police uniform there. Camaraderie was strong and, although you were on your own with just your thoughts and the general public around you for most of the time, there was always the feeling that colleagues would not let you down if you really needed them. That laudable sense of solidarity could no doubt be taken a bit too far on occasion.

One dark night a young man of aggressive demeanour was brought to the station under arrest for assaulting a policeman. The night duty sergeant, a powerfully built policeman 'of the old school' with acknowledged prowess as a wrestler and hands and feet to match, took it upon himself to administer summary justice to the miscreant there and then, on his way to confinement in the cells for the night. Having recorded the appropriate details on the station charge sheet, he set about the not noticeably repentant lad with measured slaps and blows to the body that were interspersed with the words of a lecture on the lines of 'I'll – teach – you – to – assault – policemen!' Maybe understandable, if perhaps a bit over the top since assaulting a policeman at that time was known to be treated a lot more seriously than it was in later years – and there were a few witnesses about.

When the defendant appeared before the magistrates next morning, he made no complaint about what happened to him at the police station the night before. Indeed, he said he wanted to say how well he had been treated by the police at Kendal, in contrast with his experiences some time earlier in similar circumstances at Preston in Lancashire, where they had broken his leg!

Lest it be thought that I may be some kind of closet sadist who is going to launch out on a litany of police violence for the discomfiture of readers of a nervous disposition, let me hasten to say that this activity was a rarity in my experience. While I am not inclined to condone any of it, it was most likely to occur with a detainee who was particularly truculent or aggressive and never in the case of someone who was the least bit co-operative. Then again, the police job is bound to attract the occasional individual who is handy with his fists, and such talents can sometimes come in useful of course.

My constable colleagues on beat patrol in the town varied in police service from complete beginners like me to a few of 20 or so years' experience. One stood out as something of a character. With about 20 years' service in the police and wartime experience in the forces before that, he came over as a cynical 'old sweat' who seemed to enjoy being objectionable. An intelligent man, he probably found it galling not to have a position of responsibility in the job, although it was doubtful he had ever bothered to achieve the necessary first step of passing the sergeant's promotion examination. He did have a habit of preying on probationers.

My first real encounter with the inimitable Gordon was around 6.20 one fine summer's morning. The time was more than significant because I had just a few months' police service and had slept in for early turn (6am-2pm). It was the first time I had done such a thing, and as I sprinted the mile or so to the station from my lodgings on the town outskirts, helmet in hand and hoping no one would see me, my expectation of a future in the job was running out as fast as my breath.

As I rounded the last bend and the police station came into view I was confronted by the uniformed Gordon, hands on hips and looking his most menacing. He had a habit of adopting a broad Cumbrian accent, and this morning he exercised his linguistic talent to the full. 'Where the hell's thoo bin'?

'Slept in', I replied lamely.

'Slept in? Slept in! Oh, thoo's for it,' he said.

I sort of thought that already. Anyway, I said resignedly, 'Where's the Sergeant?' I thought I might as well get it over with right away.

My 'friend' Gordon looked aghast and said 'What? Have you not seen him?'

Becoming even more alarmed, I replied, 'Well, no, should I have?'

He retorted, 'Well, he's out looking for you. And you haven't even seen him? Oh! thoo's had it.' He just turned away and walked back into the station, shaking his head sadly.

I followed Gordon inside and sat down to await the worst. It was now nearly 6.30am. There was no one else about, which was not surprising in itself because the morning shift normally consisted only of a sergeant and two constables. I was looking dejectedly out of the window when the shift sergeant pedalled round the corner on his bike.

I thought I might as well go to the door to meet the sergeant. As he came in, I thought his expression was not quite what I had been expecting. Before I had time to say anything, he said, shaking his head sadly, 'First time in 20 years.' He had slept in himself! I could not believe my luck. My relief was such that I did not even bother to remonstrate with my tormentor of a few minutes before.

In fact, I discovered subsequently that slight over-sleeping for the 6am shift seemed to happen to nearly everyone sometimes. It was a bit of a shock to the system and was never exactly condoned, but the occasional mishap of that kind usually passed off without too much fuss. It certainly was not regarded as a sacking offence, even for a probationer. In some forces, though, particularly the smaller city or borough forces without very humane regimes, lateness for duty would lead straight to an entry in the Discipline Book.

I heard later that this Gordon character had himself overslept for the 6am start a little while previously. His 'crime' had been detected by an inspector, who had come in unexpectedly at 6am, and he had been told to submit a report on the reasons for it. The duty report was neatly typed by Gordon himself, and a copy was circulating long after the event. It read much as follows:

Sir,
I have to report that I am a member of the human race. As such, I am subject to all the human frailties. This caused me this morning, I am ashamed to say, to over-sleep, with the consequence that I arrived at the police station no less than ten minutes late. I admit what I have done and am prepared to submit to any punishment that the heinousness of this offence so richly deserves.

This apparently caused a bit of a rumpus at the time but Gordon took the view that he had simply reported the facts. Nobody could ever accuse him of being a crawler. I noticed that this man did seem to enjoy exercising his literary talents and was often to be seen bending earnestly over a typewriter. I was to see him bending over prostrate policemen more than once as well.

One morning the whole division was standing stiffly to attention on the Town Hall dance floor awaiting the arrival of the H.M.I. (Her Majesty's Inspector of Constabulary), who was on his annual inspection of the force. Such events in 1963 were inclined to be very tense occasions that always included a formal parade. You could have heard a pin drop. Suddenly there was an almighty crash from just behind me. I glanced round to find that the tension had got to a very young constable who was now flat on his back on the floor. Gordon was down on one knee, bending over the young man with words of encouragement.

A couple of years later I was involved in a wholly exceptional occurrence, to become known as the Oxenholme Incident, when three policemen were shot at a railway station, one fatally. It was about 2am in the middle of a February night when a party of us who had been sent to the railway station arrived on the platform just after the shooting to find a uniformed constable lying on his back in the dim light, shouting out in pain. Gordon was already there, down on one knee beside the man and reassuring him that he 'would be at Brunton Park on Saturday' (home ground of Carlisle United Football Club, the stricken constable's local club). There will be more on this particular event later in the book.

The complement of uniform patrol staff in the town included one policewoman. This was well before the Sex Discrimination Act of course, and at this time police forces had a separate establishment for women. With no disrespect whatsoever to the ladies – quite the reverse in fact – there was no pretence in 1963 about women doing exactly the same job in the police as the men and having just the same pay and conditions. Women did shorter hours with rather less pay, and their primary role was to deal with the problems of women and children.

Also based in the town was a Traffic Section, with their cars and motorcycles, and a small band of CID men. Traffic and CID were slightly better than the beat staff because they were the specialists! Actually, not a lot of ill feeling between branches was detectable, although CID did seem – at least to a novice – to surround themselves with a little bit of mystique. Of course, they were distinguished from the rest of us by the fact that they did not wear uniform.

The first thing for a novice to learn was the beats. The town was divided up into about six beats, which seemed to have remained unaltered for years. However, you were provided with a written description of each, and naturally at first you went out with someone more experienced to learn your way round. Actually, this initial guidance was minimal and after only a matter of days you found yourself on your own to learn the job by trial and error. The process was eased a bit by putting new probationers on full nights (10pm-6am) or half nights (6pm-2am) for the first week or two so that you could find your way about without too much embarrassment with members of the public who would not have realised how lost you were yourself.

This of course was before the introduction of the personal radio. So that the sergeant or inspector would know roughly where each man should be at any particular time, the beats were on generally fixed routes and were worked in one direction only. To tie you down further, it was necessary to 'keep a point' at regular intervals. This was usually at a public telephone box, and the drill was to arrive at the 'point' five minutes before the appointed time and remain there until five minutes after it. Nine times out of ten the 'phone did not ring for you and no supervisory officer appeared there, but you could never be sure so the point had to be kept religiously. Anyway, when things were quiet it broke up what could otherwise have been a long three or four hours between starting time and 'refs' (refreshments) or 'refs' and finishing time. The routes and times tended to be so rigid that the more observant members of the public seemed able to anticipate your movements. No doubt this could have applied also to wrong-doers but I was never aware of any particular problems on that score.

In theory, beats were still 'fixed' during the day-time but in practice there was a lot more flexibility of movement. In any case, during the day, you tended to find yourself on a point of a different sort, i.e. in the middle of a road junction waving your arms at the traffic, sometimes for several hours at a stretch if there was nobody else to take over. This applied particularly to the daytime town centre beat.

Assignment to the centre beat carried the added responsibility of looking out for the blue light. About twelve or fifteen feet above street level a small blue light was attached to the wall of a building, and immediately below the light was a telephone handset in a box. If the office reserve man at the police station wanted a policeman, he could switch on the blue light to attract the attention of the town centre man, who then was expected to use the associated telephone direct line to the station. This was the only means the station had of contacting a beat man between fixed points. Again, a surprising number of observant – or perhaps just nosey – members of the public seemed to know about the blue light also and would draw your attention to the fact that the light was on before you had noticed it yourself. The antiquated system usually seemed to work well enough.

What did it feel like to appear in public in police uniform? Apart from feeling conspicuous? While you still felt the same in yourself as before, you thought instinctively that the public must expect you to be something different. Despite the cynical 'old' constable's comment in his report about being 'a member of the human race', doubts crept in the first time you had to use a public toilet in uniform and you noticed the reactions of members of the public who were using the same facilities at the time. One thing that was noticeable right away was how lonely your beat could be, even if there were a lot of people about. With no personal radios then there was no one to talk to for 99% of the time except the public. Often you hoped somebody would just ask you the time or the way to the barber or something. The relative loneliness of your position produced its own pressures to be of service and to be approachable.

Alone as you were for most of the time, you had to be resourceful and self-reliant. There was no quick way of asking for help or advice. Often it would just be a question of being asked for directions to a street or place you had never heard of, and in that case you had to be ready to admit your ignorance and ask in a nearby shop or office. I was often surprised by how naive people could be in their expectations of your range of knowledge as a policeman, with questions like 'What's early closing day in Bristol?' or 'When is the next bus to Windermere?' or even, on one occasion, 'Can you give me directions to London?' (250 miles away and before there was much of a motorway network).

Needless to say, there was always a healthy sense of vulnerability as well. You quickly found out, if you didn't know already, that there was nothing to be gained by rushing in or throwing you weight about. Why not take it slowly or keep out of it altogether if the problem was soon going to sort itself out anyway? Tact and discretion were often forced upon you, and abandon them at your peril!

Making an arrest on the street tended to be something of a last resort, when you couldn't think of any other way out. I remember the momentous occasion of my first arrest without warrant. The individual concerned was obviously tired and lonely and had nowhere to go for the night so he swung his bag round his head and flung it through the plate glass window of a shop on the main street. Getting him to go to the station and giving him a cell for the night was no problem.

Slightly more difficult was the drunk who staggered up to me one night and told me he was going to 'knock my block off.' We discussed his proposal without achieving any change of mind on his part, so eventually I negotiated a deal whereby we would sort it out a couple of hundred yards up the road where no one else was likely to be offended by the spectacle. He hardly seemed to notice as he was bundled the last few yards into the police station. The gentleman appeared in court next day and was fined ten shillings (50 pence) for being drunk and disorderly. No doubt justice was done. Anyway, it took me out of the cold for a while and got me the kudos of an arrest without warrant. They did keep a check on the reports you put in and the incidents you dealt with.

Making arrests, though, was certainly not a priority, There was little or no feeling of Police v Public, and arrests were not happening all the time. When dealing with drunks it often seemed better just to get them off the street for their own safety, without all the trouble of getting them to the police station (where they might make a mess in a cell). In any case, there was no way of contacting the police station for help, except by telephone, and there was no van on call for carrying difficult prisoners to the station.

If you did find a 'phone, you were liable to find that there was no one to help you anyway, except the man who answered the 'phone. He could not leave the station because he was on his own there, so it was likely to be some time before he could get anyone else to you (by switching on the town centre blue light or contacting someone else by 'phone at his hour-end point).

So you just had to be resourceful and work it out for yourself. If it was a warm night when you encountered a drunk, why not get him into a shop doorway or onto a sheltered park bench if there was one handy? On one occasion an obliging taxi-driver stopped as I was dealing with a drunk and took him home for me. One night I found a young woman lying on the street very much the worse for drink. She was able to tell me where she lived and it was not all that far away so I simply picked her up and half-carried, half-walked her there. (Back at the station later that night I found that somebody had reported seeing a policeman on the street in uniform with his arm around a young woman. It must have looked a bit funny but I thought it was the right thing to do at the time).

What was much more common at this time was the need to deal with drivers for parking offences. There were no traffic wardens to do the dirty work then and no yellow lines at the kerb edge to indicate exactly where it was not permissible to park. The offence of 'unnecessary obstruction' was a common one, often through a driver leaving his vehicle in a position where it obstructed access to an alleyway leading to the rear of premises.

Parking without lights was another one because in 1963 there was no legal provision whereby a vehicle could be left unlit in a speed restricted area. Vehicles left on a road after dark always had to show lights. Actually, my very first offence report was for an unlit vehicle. I was told by the sergeant how to go about it, and I do not know who was the more nervous at the time – me or the unfortunate car driver. Often, of course, it was sufficient just to point out the offence and leave it at that, but it was necessary to submit an offence report in cases that seemed in your judgement to be the more blatant, or perhaps where more than one offence was revealed at the same time.

One night very early on in my experience I had a really desperate case of two offences at the same time – bike without lights the wrong way up a one-way street. When I stopped the lad he did not look at all concerned about his transgressions, which he readily admitted. However, he refused to give me his name and address so I was stuck and simply had to let him go. Feeling slightly peeved by the young man's cocky attitude, I made careful note of his appearance and the direction of his departure from the scene.

On return to the station later that night, I told the shift sergeant what had happened. The description fitted a young man of his acquaintance and it was decided that justice had to be done. By about 3am the sergeant and I were knocking at the door of a darkened house just off the main street. Amid some verbal abuse from the middle-aged lady who eventually appeared at an upstairs window we discovered we were at the right house (fortunately, I suppose, in the circumstances).

The young cyclist was duly roused from his bed and told he would be reported for the two aforementioned offences.

It turned out he was on leave from the Army abroad so the processes were speeded up for him and a summons was prepared for his appearance in court within two days. As we left the house the distraught mother shouted after us, 'It was you lot that drove him into the Army anyway!'

Normally the decision whether to report or not was your own, but occasionally as a probationer you would be told by a supervisory officer to put in an offence report that you were not happy about. The doubtful cases were always trivial matters, and I was inclined to remember the fair treatment I had always had from policemen I had encountered before joining the job myself. In fact, but for their fairness I might have 'had a record' that would have prevented me getting in the job at all.

Then again, I felt I was mature enough to make up my own mind in minor matters and was always conscious of the fact that, in the event of a not guilty plea, it would be me that would have to justify my action before the magistrates, not the sergeant or the inspector who had told me to get my pocket book out. The witness box can be an uncomfortable place if your heart is not in what you have done. Anyway, the problem did not arise very often. The regime was generally fair in this way as in others.

Attendance at road accidents was naturally something that fell to your lot from time to time. Most were minor but occasionally you could find yourself with a nasty one. Experience quickly showed, though, that the basics were the same in all cases and it was all down to a matter of priorities – protect the scene first, see to any casualties, make a note of any witnesses, remove the obstruction and so on. The problems usually arose afterwards when it came to taking statements and sorting out the paperwork.

The administrative follow-up was always the most difficult part in my view. And it always surprised me how often someone would turn up to help you with problems at the scene – perhaps even a nurse or doctor if you were lucky. Nevertheless, the first road accident I had to deal with was probably a mess on my part even though it only involved a heavy goods vehicle knocking down some traffic lights. Again, of course, there was no easy way of getting help, and it was all down to the individual at the scene. I believe at the time I felt like removing my helmet and mingling with the crowd. It got sorted out eventually and I learned a lot from it.

I thought 'domestics' (attendance at domestic disputes) were as perplexing as anything. It always struck me as terribly sad that the most private and personal of problems should reach the stage where there were uniformed strangers in the house. Some cases of course were well-known 'regulars' but not all by any means, and there was usually nothing much the police could do in such a situation, despite what well-meaning people seem to think these days. About the only thing you could do with a 'domestic' was listen for a reasonable time, making the odd inoffensive comment now and then, and hope you could leave the house a little bit better than you found it.

Any positive action was likely to be counter-productive. However bad the atmosphere at 11pm when the husband had just got in from the pub, you had no means of knowing what it would be like next morning. And the chances were that the parties were going to carry on living together so there was not much point in making a big issue out of these things or bothering yourself about possible proceedings that were likely to end up without a written complaint. And yet these issues are still very much a police function, and rightly so.

One fatal road accident I attended had a particularly poignant twist to it. A middle-aged couple had been travelling in their car along an unlit country road in heavy rain when they hit a flooded section of road that the driver clearly had not seen in time. The car went off to the offside of the road and collided head-on with a bus coming the other way, ending up under its front overhang. The car was wrecked and both occupants must have died instantly.

I had only been back at the station a few minutes when the 'phone rang. It was a young man's voice. He said his father and mother had left their home a couple of hours earlier to come and visit him but they had not arrived. He wondered if we knew of them having any problems with their car. There were two or three of us in the office at the time who had been at the scene of the accident and we looked at each other in silence for a moment. The caller was put through to the inspector. Inquiries of this nature are quite common but usually it is possible to assure the caller you know nothing about it. This was a particularly tragic exception in my experience.

Attendance at post mortem examinations was something that seemed to crop up quite a lot. Any sudden death where a doctor could not issue a certificate as to the cause had to be reported to the Coroner. The police were involved in such cases as coroner's officers, and if a post mortem was ordered then the reporting officer had to attend it. I suppose you would not have been there by choice but it was part of the job so it just had to be faced. Actually, I found it best just to take a few deep breaths afterwards as you walked out into the fresh air and then go and have a good meal as soon as possible. After that forget about it.

The good doctor who was our regular pathologist had a very calm and matter-of-fact manner as he went about his unenviable task, and this helped a lot to lighten the atmosphere at such events. As a policeman you were there mainly to identify the body to the pathologist and tell him at first hand what you knew of the circumstances, but one particular pathologist would have you rather more involved in proceedings by handing him instruments and so on. In one case of apparent suicide by gassing he even had me bending closely over the body's exposed lungs and sniffing for gas.

One memorable night all these elements of patrolling alone on foot without a personal radio, the fatal accident and the trip to the mortuary combined to produce an embarrassing situation for me. It was about 3am on a warm summer's night and the streets were very quiet. Then I noticed a stationary car with two shadowy figures in it just off the main street. The young man in the driver's seat did everything right on the face of it. He said it was his car, he gave me the correct registration number without getting out to look and he rhymed off the name and address on the driving licence he produced as I was holding it in my hand. He and his young male companion gave me plausible explanations of what they were doing there, but somehow I was just not satisfied and told them we were going to the police station for further checks. They did not argue. I got in the back seat of the car in all my majesty and was driven the mile or so to the police station.

As we drew up at the front door the night sergeant rushed out. There was obviously something on. I started to explain my problem but he broke in with the news that there had been a 'double fatal' (road accident with two dead) and he and I had to get ourselves up to the hospital mortuary pronto. When I protested about my two suspects, the hard-bitten old sergeant – a new arrival in the town who did not seem too happy with his enforced move here – spoke very briefly with them and then told me to 'give them a chit for their documents and chase them.'

Resignedly, I made out a form HORT/1 for production of insurance and test certificate and gave it to the driver who had waited quietly and patiently while I had my rather one-sided dispute with the sergeant. The sergeant and I then proceeded to the mortuary where we dealt with two bodies that I could not help thinking would not have minded waiting a little while for us to make a couple of 'phone calls about the car and the two occupants. However, it was soon 6am and I went off to my lodgings to bed.

When I reported back to the police station at 10pm that same day, I was met by the inspector who was quite clearly less than pleased with me. The car I had checked and travelled in the previous night had been found by its owner about 100 yards away from the place where he had parked it the night before in Blackpool and it had another couple of hundred miles or so on the 'clock'. Not only that but my HORT/1 form was lying on the floor.

The two lads I had had at the police station had stolen the car and the driving licence, and it transpired that that was not all they were suspected of by any means. I had the rather galling task of submitting a detailed report that had to steer a diplomatic course between exculpating myself and incriminating the rough-hewn sergeant. (After all, I was still a probationer, but the incident would have looked good on my record if it had been dealt with properly and might even have got me an official Commendation).

The Waterside Hotel, as it was known locally, was a common lodging house down by the river that attracted its nightly quota of down-and-outs and roadsters. It was a dilapidated building like something out of Dickens that was run by a sort of bespectacled Quasimodo. Checking it for possible customers of interest was a regular police task at that time, although it was demolished, like many other old properties in that part of the town, in the mid-1960s. I remember calling at the unsavoury place early one morning and finding the Quasimodo fellow using an axe in the kitchen as a tin-opener. The only other items discernible in the semi-darkness of the room were a dirty old gas cooker and a rusty old motorbike. It was not the place to linger.

As often as not, the night shift passed off so quietly that you tended to wish something would happen to liven things up a bit. Shaking hands with all the shop door handles on your beat was the primary task after the streets had gone quiet; 99% of business people would have locked up before they left for the day but occasionally a door would unexpectedly open as you tried it and you would almost fall in. In these cases the key-holder was asked to attend and check the premises before they were secured. Not all key-holders were pleased to be dragged out of bed for this purpose. No doubt gratitude was too much to expect in these circumstances but they were probably more careful in future.

Until just before this time the police station had held keys to all the business and commercial premises in the town. This system was ended suddenly when a young policeman got four years' imprisonment for large-scale thefts from insecure shops while on night duty – a bad business that was a public talking-point some time after the event. Incidentally, it was said at the police station that the culprit's last probationer report before all this came to light had included the supervisor's assessment – 'Not bright, but honest as the day is long!' That comment remained in the back of my mind years later when I had the job of doing probationer reports myself.

The night shift was sometimes enlivened by the appearance out of the gloom of one of the town's 'characters'. Prominent among them was Jimmy, a man aged 40 or so whose problems and those of his family were well known to the Social Services Department of the local authority (or Welfare Department, as it was called then). Jimmy and his long-suffering wife lived happily with their dog in appalling squalor in a caravan parked in a secluded lane just outside the town. He seemed to have a knack of turning up at your point late at night and engaging you in earnest conversation on local affairs, and he was not averse to using the 'secret' police 'phone below the town centre blue light to contact the station, if the mood or the drink so took him.

'Kendal Mary' was a lady of the night who was always beautifully turned out, a striking figure with the upswept blonde hair, the fur coat and the well groomed white poodle on a lead. She might have been past the first flush of youth but she was far more presentable and personable than other 'diesel queens' on our part of the A6 trunk road who plied their trade for the benefit of lorry drivers far from home. One night in the small hours she turned up in the town centre, immaculate as ever but minus her poodle, and started to engage me in earnest conversation just as a large Jaguar car drew up at the kerbside.

The male driver, who was on his own, leaned out to ask me for directions to a filling station for petrol, and I started to give the man appropriate advice. Mary interposed with an offer to show the man the way herself, and elegantly got in the car without waiting for a response from the driver. The passenger door closed behind her and the car swept off south. This Jaguar must have been quite a change for Mary from the cab of an eight-wheeler, although what the car driver thought of police service in these parts and local hospitality is anybody's guess.

Frankie was a local ne'er-do-well who kept turning up when things were quiet and wanting to ingratiate himself. He lived with his family in an awful little hovel just off the main street. The town at that time had a maze of alleyways leading off the main street, and these were full of old houses that were demolished in the 1960s and 70s to make way for car parks and such like.

Being called one dark night to Frankie's unsavoury

residence, I found it had been the scene of a particularly violent 'domestic'. A woman was sitting among the wreckage with a heavily bloodstained towel around her head and there were bloodstains all over the wallpaper. She had apparently had a plate smashed over her head and the pieces were lying about the floor. However, after taking the 'minimum action necessary to secure the objective' (whatever that was in this case), I left them to it. It was no doubt their way of life and nothing was going to alter it. Incidentally, Frankie got six months' imprisonment soon after this for assaulting a police colleague called to one of his tantrums. (No messing about with suspended sentences or £50 fines for assault on police in those days).

By far my most memorable night in the police at this time (or at any other time for that matter) was one where I should not have been on duty at all – and I certainly never got paid for it. For me it was a date to remember.

It was 9 February 1965. I was just going off duty and leaving the station at 6pm when a car was reported stolen from the town. While I made a mental note of the registration number, I did not take much interest because I was looking forward to a week's leave that was starting just then. I had much more important matters on my mind as well, particularly the girlfriend I was seeing that evening. I went back to my lodgings on the town's outskirts and forgot about it.

Just before midnight that same day I was in my old Ford car, saying goodnight to my girlfriend outside her home in the town, when there was a knock on the window. It was one of my on-duty colleagues. Thinking he was just taking the mickey, I wound down the window and started to tell him to clear off. However, he looked serious. He told me that an armed man had fired shots at policemen in the town earlier that evening and he was believed to be still in the area. A big search was getting under way. It turned out later that it was the same man who had earlier taken the car.

I dropped off my girlfriend and shot straight up the road to my digs to get changed back into uniform, (maybe I should have got into bed but I didn't want to miss anything). My haste to join the fray was such that I just put on my outer police uniform and forgot I was still wearing a green shirt and tie.

Reporting back to the station as soon as I could, I found people milling about everywhere. Some sort of order emerged out of the chaos, and I found myself with a party assigned to search the bottom end of the town where there were a couple of football pitches and a cricket field with buildings that might have provided cover for the fugitive. One or two of us had been issued with firearms but most of us were unarmed. As we groped about in the darkness I picked up a large stone that I thought would be better than nothing as a missile if I needed one. I had picked up my torch as I left my digs but of course it was impossible to use it for fear of attracting the attention of an individual who was obviously not averse to using a gun on the police.

I suppose in situations of danger you tend to feel that the worst is something that happens to somebody else but not you. But such an incident as this, with an armed man on the loose and so many firearms being carried openly by the police, was something that I had never expected to be involved in so early in my police career in rural Westmorland. Subsequent press coverage was enormous and television carried shots of uniformed policemen carrying firearms for the first time that I could remember.

After an unsuccessful search of the south end of the town I was back at the police station around 2am, when word came in of shots being fired at Oxenholme Railway Station on the main line about two miles away. When a large group of us got there soon afterwards we found a desperate scene.

Three policemen had been shot, and an ambulance was just leaving with two of them while the third was still lying on his back on the station platform, obviously in a lot of pain, with a uniformed colleague kneeling beside him. It turned out that the three men, an inspector and two constables from Carlisle, had encountered the gunman in the station waiting room. All three had been hit and both constables were badly injured. One of them died soon afterwards, I'm afraid.

I suppose nowadays the police would have backed off at that and simply waited for the specialist firearms teams to arrive. At that time, however, there was no such team, and there had never been any real planning for such an occurrence as this in our part of the world. We simply carried on searching the railway station area. The whole thing had an air of unreality about it. It was the middle of a February night on what would normally have been a deserted railway station, and yet there were policemen everywhere in the dim light and there were the agonized shouts of the man lying injured on the platform. The overnight main line trains were still running, and it was not long before a steam-hauled express tore through the station at about 80 miles an hour with a tremendous crash of noise and disappeared south into the darkness.

It soon became clear that our man had gone. I joined a group of about ten others and we started to follow the railway line northwards. Again, there was the fear of using a torch because this man was clearly in the vicinity, and we were stumbling over things in the darkness. We veered off the main line to the left, down the branch line towards Kendal. There were a few firearms among us but I was encumbered with a heavy radio pack which never worked, either to transmit or receive, so we were completely out of touch with what was going on elsewhere.

Eventually we covered the couple of miles or so to the town along the railway line and reported back to the police station. Reinforcements were now arriving, not only from other parts of our area but from other police forces as well. There were road blocks everywhere, dawn was breaking and traffic was starting to pile up. By about 8am I found myself on point duty in the town main street. It was chaotic. By 9am I was relieved on the point, and soon afterwards I managed to get myself back to the digs and into bed. I had been more or less continuously on the go for over 24 hours and was absolutely done in.

The murderer was captured later that same day. Soon after I had got to bed he was spotted with his gun out in the country just outside the town, and the chase ended when he was brought down by a rifle shot in the leg by a friend of mine who was normally on traffic patrol. He then shot himself in the head. While neither the police bullet nor his own proved fatal, the effect of the latter was to render him unfit to plead at his trial for murder and he was committed to a secure mental institution.

Two policemen of my acquaintance later received bravery awards for trying to arrest this armed man early on in the course of the incident, when he had fired shots at them in the town and got away. I recall standing next to one of these two men at a rather chaotic briefing at which firearms were being handed out. No disrespect to the rather elderly superintendent, who no doubt was as unfamiliar with such an occurrence as we all were, but I did think his final comment of 'Now don't shoot him' was a bit 'naff' in the circumstances. Having just been issued with a revolver and still feeling the effects of being shot at only a few hours earlier, my constable friend next to me put it in perspective when he muttered, 'I'll shoot the bastard if I get sight of him'.

Of the three policemen – the inspector and two constables –

who were shot at the railway station, one of the constables died in hospital an hour or so later. The other constable survived, although he was badly injured and destined to be pensioned off the job. The inspector was not badly hurt and returned to duty at Carlisle soon afterwards. He did in fact transfer to Kendal some years later on promotion to superintendent, although unfortunately I have to record that he shot himself dead in the police station armoury only a few weeks after his promotion. The Oxenholme incident was mentioned at the inquest as a possible factor that had preyed on his mind.

Back to everyday matters. It was approaching spring and I learned that a temporary addition to staff was needed on the local Traffic section to help with the anticipated increase in summer traffic in this area of the southern Lake District. I understood two motorcyclists were required. I put in an application by way of a report on my previous motorcycling experience that caused the sergeant who submitted it through the channels to comment that if all this lot was right, I should have been on Traffic Patrol before I ever joined the police force! Incidentally, this particular gentleman, worldly-wise as he was, had a philosophical view of things that rather stuck in my mind and was summed up nicely in his remark that 'the police job would be all right if it wasn't for policemen.' I sometimes reflected on that in later years.

Anyway, my application for Traffic was successful. I was keen to stay on at Kendal for personal as well as job-related reasons, after my two-year probationary period, and I thought this secondment to Traffic would be one way of extending my stay by about six months at least. I understood there had been only one other applicant for these two jobs so I thought I was safe. As it happened, two others were interested. The good news was that we were all successful but the bad news for me was that my two associates were staying at Kendal while I was on my way up the A6 road to force headquarters at Penrith where they also wanted extra motorcyle cover.

Ah well, no turning back now. I did about a week's course with the force motorcycle instructor and was raring to go. I had not ridden a motorbike for a year or so but of course the technique soon came back. The only problem was the elderly machine they lent me for the introductory course was a pensioned-off patrol bike with a particularly disconcerting habit of sending nasty electric shocks through the handlebars when it rained – which was often. However, I passed the course and was confident in the belief that I would be allocated a proper police bike like the ones you saw on the recruiting posters of the time. (Still an optimist, with just over two years' service.)

3
HEADQUARTERS TRAFFIC PATROL

The smiling uniformed sergeant who welcomed me to the Traffic Patrol at police headquarters near Penrith that early spring morning in 1965 offered a reassuring first impression of my new department. But he seemed to have been taken by surprise. He did not really know why I was there, and my name did not appear on his duty sheets. He promised to put that right and fix me up with some duty times.

Next to the stores where long-serving storeman Ernie was far more organised. Unlike the control room sergeant, he actually knew I was coming. Not only that, he had put aside a set of motor cycle kit; indeed, it appeared to be the only set he had. I was soon kitted out with a white helmet that was rather too small, a Barbour-style waxed cotton jacket that was a bit on the big side, a pair of riding breeches that were too tight and a pair of heavy duty motor cycle boots that were a couple of sizes too big. All of it looked distinctly second-hand but the choice was simply 'Take it or leave it'. I had to take it.

The confusing welcome to the Traffic Department and the ill-fitting old kit were just softeners-up for the next confrontation – the Bike. The charmless garage sergeant, who clearly had no interest in motor cycles anyway, presented me with a black 650cc BSA that was to be my steed for the foreseeable future. It looked so far from new that I wondered if the 40-odd thousand miles showing on the 'clock' were genuine or whether it had been round more than once – or perhaps the speedometer had been replaced at some time. I never did find out. It looked pretty rough. Again, however, there was no choice. It was the only one available.

The next job was to get a radio fitted to the bike. Harry, the resident Home Office wireless man soon fixed me up with a standard police motor cycle radio that plugged in behind the single saddle. A quick test call and all seemed well. Spirits were rising. Incidentally, experience was to show that the radio on a police motorcycle was a vital piece of equipment, so it was as well to keep up a good relationship with the man whose job it was to look after it for you. Even sounder considerations of self-interest applied to one's dealings with Jakob, the temperamental ex-German prisoner-of-war who did the routine maintenance on the motorcycles. It turned out that Jackie, as he was known, was inclined to mete out retribution for any perceived slight in the form of a marked reluctance to take an interest in one's bike. In the little hierarchy that was HQ Traffic he had somehow managed to establish a status of his own as something of a law unto himself.

Eventually, however, with duties worked out for the week ahead and a patrol area allocated for the rest of the first day, I was ready to roll. The kit didn't fit too well and the bike looked a bit depressing but I thought it would be a wolf in sheep's clothing – after all it was a police bike. It said so on the big white fairing that graced the front of the machine. Well, it was a sort of off-white anyway, being somewhat affected by age and weathering.

I got the full weight of the ill-fitting right boot on the kick-starter (no soppy starter buttons on motorcycles in those days) and started the engine. The bike felt as heavy as lead and a blip of the throttle suggested the pistons were made of the same material. Throttle response was decidedly unenthusiastic. Once under way, the bike seemed distinctly under-powered for its weight. I had recently owned a 650cc Triumph twin myself and mental comparison of the two suggested that the BSA ran about as well as the Triumph with one plug lead removed. Its best cruising speed seemed to be no more than 50mph and after that the engine vibration got rather nasty. At 70-ish it was so bad the landscape became blurred. I imagined the effect to be something like that of using a pneumatic drill on a hard road surface. Still, with a small patrol area to cover there should be no need for speed anyway, otherwise you would have got to the far end of your area too quickly.

I soon found the radio could be something of a problem. The bike only had a six-volt electrical system, charged by a dynamo, and it didn't really seem able to keep up with the demands of the radio unless the engine was kept running for much of the time. The radio had a Receive-Only mode in addition to Receive and Transmit, and if left in the former the set caused less drain on the battery. The snag was, the radio then took a while to warm up sufficiently to transmit when switched over to the other mode so there was some delay in replying if Control was calling you while you were on Receive Only. Not all the radio operators seemed to know about this problem, and they were inclined to give up waiting for you to reply while you were still waiting for the set to warm up. Then again, the range of the radio was limited. From a hill-top it might be at least twenty miles but this could be drastically reduced if there was a hill between you and the transmitter. The worst problem, though, seemed to be the engine's vibration. At low speed it did little harm but one quick burst at 60 or 70mph with all rivets seemingly vibrating could leave you with a dead radio. This could have embarrassing consequences, as I was soon to find out.

At this time the HQ Traffic Patrol staff consisted of about a dozen car drivers and four motorcyclists. Motorcycles worked mainly day shifts but every fourth week there was a full week of night duty (10pm-6am) in the force control room. There was no point in turning out motor cyclists on

Carleton Hall, near Penrith, photographed in 1930s. The building has been Cumbria Police Headquarters since the 1950s.

nights because naturally the main advantage of a two-wheeler – its manoeuvrability in traffic – disappeared when traffic was light. Also the six-volt lighting system fitted to the old BSAs was hardly safe outside a well-lit built-up area.

The allocated patrol area consisted of twenty miles or so of A6 and A66 trunk road, and it soon became clear that a regular task was escorting abnormal loads, particularly through the old town of Penrith but also on the open road outside the town in the case of very large or slow moving vehicles. There was rather more to it than just riding slowly ahead of the mobile obstacle. The main thing was to know the road ahead and make sure you got to the far side of any narrow sections well before the load got there so that you could get oncoming traffic stopped in good time. The drivers of these loads were remarkably good and we had an excellent working relationship with them. This was before there were any motorways or dual carriageways in the Penrith area, and the locality's ancient road system was never designed for the sort of vehicles we regularly escorted.

I never had any serious mishaps involving an abnormal load, although once or twice there were incidents like shop blinds being carried away. Anything that went wrong had to be down to the lorry driver, but as escort you did feel a keen sense of responsibility to make sure everything went right until you got him away off your patch.

Escorting abnormal loads through the town soon brought me up against the sometimes slightly uneasy relationship between the town police staff and the traffic patrol based a mile or so away at force headquarters. There was a width limit of 12' 6' (3.81m) on vehicles that could be taken through the streets. I was instructed by control one day to pick up a southbound abnormal load that was awaiting escort through the built-up area. I thought it looked well up to the width limit and had no doubt it would go through the Narrows in the town centre so I set off south with the vehicle behind me. I had only gone about half a mile when I was confronted by the town police inspector.

Obviously he had heard on the town police station VHF radio the instruction to me to take the wide load through the town and had dashed out on to the main street to ambush me. Anyway, he stopped me in my tracks and told me to 'Take the bloody thing out again!' I had to manoeuvre the load round and travel back the way I had come in order to go round the outskirts – all hills and tight corners and about four miles longer than the direct route through the town centre. (This particular inspector was supposed to have applied once to join the traffic patrol and been turned down, leaving him with a grudge against traffic police).

It wasn't all a case of escorting slow-moving abnormal loads, even though that chore seemed about all the cumbersome vibrating old BSA seemed fit for. On my very first Bank Holiday Monday out on traffic patrol I was travelling sedately south-east down the A66 road, a few miles from base at Police Headquarters. It was late afternoon, the road was quiet, the sun was still warm and I was thinking to myself, 'By Jove, I get paid for this.'

Suddenly I noticed an oncoming car flashing its headlights. The signal was clearly meant for me and the car was stopping at the roadside. I went across to the other side of the road and stopped beside the car, which contained a man and a woman. The male driver exclaimed, 'There's a car in front of us and the driver's all over the road.'

I asked my informant to follow me and set off up the road at a pace that the old bike had probably not experienced for years. After about three miles of vibro-massage, I came up behind a large Ford car. It was travelling quite slowly and veering from side to side, occasionally coming into contact with the roadside hedge and sending up tufts of grass and dandelions. I kept a cautious distance astern and watched. The driver was wearing a wide-brimmed hat like a Stetson and his male passenger's head was slumped back against the seat. Both looked drunk to me.

Perched vulnerably on the bike, I could not safely get past the car for a while. Eventually the car slowed to negotiate an 'S' bend at a river bridge, which it crossed without hitting anything. As the road straightened out after the bridge, I saw my chance and nipped past on the approach to a large lay-by. Keeping a safe distance ahead of the car and being ready to accelerate away if necessary, I started slowing the car down with the appropriate left hand signal to the driver. He appeared to understand what I wanted him to do.

I noticed that an old black Ford 'Popular' car was already parked on the lay-by, about half way along it. As soon as I was satisfied that my friend in the large Ford car knew I wanted him to stop on the lay-by behind the 'Pop', I went past the little car and stopped just in front of it. Ever cautious, I wanted something between my drunken friend and my rear, if indeed he had not got the message. Clearly however, he had.

I dismounted and headed back to the large Ford. As I walked past the little Ford 'Pop' I noticed there was a man sitting in the driver's seat. His window was open and his elbow rested on the window ledge. He just glanced at me as I walked past.

One look in the big Ford was enough to convince me that both the driver and his passenger were well under the influence. I reached into the car and took the ignition key from the switch, telling the driver to stay where he was. As I turned to go back to the motor cycle I noticed that my informant and his lady passenger by now were also arriving on the lay-by and parking at a respectful distance behind the big Ford. There was now quite a little convoy of vehicles standing on the lay-by, with my motor cycle at the front, the Ford 'Pop' (with driver) just behind it, then the car with the two drunks and finally the informant's car with two occupants.

I used my machine's radio to call for assistance in the form of a car to take the drunk driver to the police station. Surprisingly this time the radio worked, which it did not always do after a high-speed run and the resulting vibration from the engine. However, I was only about a mile from base and my request was acknowledged at once.

I turned to go back to the big Ford. In the minute or so that had elapsed while I was using the radio, the scene on the lay-by had altered somewhat. The drunk driver by now had got out of his car and walked to the front off-side of the Ford 'Pop', where he was relieving himself in no uncertain fashion against the bonnet while the man sitting in the driving seat of the little car looked on in amazement and the two people in the rearmost car watched in some apparent amusement – particularly the wife, I rather thought.

There was no stopping the drunk until he was ready. I could not help wondering for a moment about the attitude of the man whose car was being defiled in this way. He just sat still and watched from a distance of about three feet without doing or saying anything.

The patrol car soon arrived on the scene and the drunk was put into it, together with his passenger who was too far gone to know what was happening. After securing their car for collection later and taking details from the two people

Austin patrol car near Penrith in the 1950s.

who had drawn my attention to what was going on, I travelled the mile or so to the police station.

As I was completing the drunk-driver formalities at the police station I noticed a man outside the charge office who seemingly had also been arrested and was waiting to be processed. He looked vaguely familiar. As I was about to leave, I approached this man and asked where I had seen him before. He said, 'I was the driver of the Ford Popular that was pee'd over down the road.' Rather surprised but with recognition dawning, I asked the man what he was doing at the police station under arrest, and he replied, 'Well, I had stolen the licence on the car.' I could not help but ask what he thought was happening when I suddenly appeared on the lay-by in front of him. He said, 'I thought you'd come for me.'

It transpired that a colleague had arrested the licence thief soon after I had left the scene with my drunk-driver, although I never found out how the offence had come to light. It seemed to me that if I really had had my wits about me I would have had two completely separate arrests for different offences at the same spot, but in the circumstances that would have been rather too much to expect. The second man's guilty secret, however, certainly explained why he had sat motionless and silent while the drunk had urinated copiously over the front of his car.

The drunk driver eventually pleaded guilty at court and was dealt with without the need for me or my two witnesses to give evidence. He had had a lot to drink that day, quite obviously; 1965 was pre-breathalyser and it was best only to arrest for drink-driving when a driver was clearly very adversely affected, otherwise there would be difficulties at court, especially if the case came before a jury. (An old superintendent of my acquaintance used to tell the story of the jury who acquitted a driver of being under the influence of alcohol but added a rider to the effect that they thought he should really not have been driving when he had had so much to drink!). There but for the grace…

Round about this time I had a number of arrests for drink-driving and never had to justify my actions in court for any of them because the drivers concerned all pleaded guilty. They had all clearly had a lot to drink and at least one was virtually paralytic.

One evening I had to respond to a complaint about a main road being blocked by a stationary car in the middle of it. I travelled the five miles or so to the scene and found that traffic had indeed been stopped by a large Jaguar car that was stationary on a hill at an angle across the middle of the road. At first sight there was no one in the car but in fact I found the sole male occupant sprawled across the back seat in a stupor. The police car driver who arrived in response to my call for assistance helped me to lift the man into the police vehicle. It appeared to be a combination of drink and drugs in his case.

In my experience at this time, drivers of heavy lorries could be the worst offenders where drink was concerned. One day, about noon, I was stationary in a police Land Rover on the A6 road a few miles south of Penrith when I got a radio call about a lorry travelling south out of the town. The vehicle was said to be veering all over the road and the driver was believed to be drunk.

I took up a position in a lay-by facing south, where I got out and stood beside the Land Rover. A couple of minutes later a lorry appeared, coming quite slowly towards me round a corner about 300 yards away. I put up my right hand in a 'Stop' signal and stepped into the roadway – but not too far! As the lorry trundled towards me, I realised it was not going to stop and got out of the way. As the lorry went past the driver looked as if he was oblivious to my presence. I jumped back in the Land Rover (feeling glad for once that I was not on two wheels), reported by radio what the situation was and set off south in pursuit. After a couple of miles I managed to get the 'White Elephant', as our only traffic patrol Land Rover was aptly called, past the slow-moving lorry. There was an old quarry at the side of the road a mile ahead, so I planned to try and get him stopped there. This was about a mile short of the next village.

Having got in front of the lorry, I put on the blue light and 'Police - Stop' sign and started slowing down gradually, at the same time keeping a wary eye on the bulky vehicle in the mirror. In fact the driver had got the message this time. He slowed down steadily and followed me off the carriageway and into the abandoned quarry, where he stopped. Feeling fairly sure that the lorry was not going to set off again, I got out of the Land Rover and went back.

I pulled open the cab door and got the driver out. He was in a state of near-stupor, and it seemed amazing that he had been able to drive at all. There were beer bottles lying all over the cab floor, some opened and some not. All good evidence and again no trouble at court. I was lucky again.

It was the old heap of a motor cycle that seemed to bring me all the luck at this time in the sense of involvement in the more 'exciting' things like making arrests for drink-driving or car theft or whatever.

One June day about 4.30pm I was on the motorcycle on the main A6 road between Carlisle and Penrith, which carried a lot of long-distance traffic and had a bad accident record at that time. While I was never one for reporting people for relatively trivial offences, I saw a Rolls Royce car travel over the crest of a hill for about 200 yards, completely on the wrong side of double white lines. It was a rather blatant breach, so I went after the Rolls and stopped it a couple of miles or so down the road. I told the driver what I had seen and informed him he would be reported for summons. It only took me a couple of minutes to take the necessary details and then I was on my way.

It was now about quarter to five and I was on the 9am-5pm shift, so with a few miles to go to base I did not hang about. There was no paid overtime then and I did not want to be late finishing. About five miles from headquarters, I was nipping smartly past the traffic when I came up behind a large articulated lorry carrying a load of steel girders. If it had been travelling in a normal manner I would have no doubt overtaken it and gone on my way. However, it wasn't moving normally but was travelling quite fast and veering all over the road – an alarming sight.

Eventually I managed to get past the lorry and prepared to stop it on a lay-by about a mile ahead. The lorry probably weighed at least 30 tons so I was being more than cautious. However, keeping well ahead of the vehicle and slowing down gradually, with measured and exaggerated left arm movements, I was clearly getting my intentions over to the driver. The lay-by was on an up-gradient which probably helped as well. Anyway, the vehicle was slowing down and at last it stopped, partly on the lay-by and partly on the road-way.

I got the bike on the stand and went back to the lorry. The driver jumped out of the cab and staggered into the road. Traffic was quite heavy. I eased the man back into the side and went back to the bike to ask for assistance to take the driver to the town police station. He had obviously had a lot to drink – no need for a breathalyser to establish that, even if such a thing had existed at the time.

When I picked up the bike's radio handset and called control, there was no response. Clearly, they were not receiving me. What had happened no doubt was that the old motor cycle's vibration in the fastish run I had done over the last few miles had simply rendered the radio inoperative. I was effectively on my own with a drunken lorry driver and his badly placed vehicle three miles from 'home'. I had the rather embarrassing experience of having to stop a passing car driver and ask him to go to a 'phone box a couple of miles down the road and dial 999 for me. Fortunately he clearly understood what I wanted and cooperated by doing what I asked, because within ten minutes or so a police car was on the scene and the lorry driver was on his way to the station.

Among the formalities at the police station there was the need to contact the lorry's owners to tell them where the vehicle and its load were. As usual in these cases the call meant instant dismissal for the lorry driver. This was tough no doubt, but this man was so drunk he could not walk straight and he had been driving a heavy vehicle towards a busy town and could have killed a lot of people.

Having dealt with the lorry driver at the town police station, I made my way back to my base at police headquarters about a mile away. On leaving my bike in the garage I was not able to report by radio that I had finished duty so it was necessary to walk across to the control room and tell them. I had already explained by telephone from the police station that I would be an hour late finishing. As I walked into the control room I was confronted by the control inspector. A well-intentioned man, although perhaps not everyone's idea of a good practical copper (whatever that may be), he looked very concerned as he said, 'So you've reported the driver of a Rolls Royce?' I confirmed that and he said no more. There was no mention of the desperately drunken heavy goods vehicle driver.

As mentioned earlier, we motor cyclists based at police headquarters were required to park up our mounts every fourth week and do a seven-night stint in the force control

Cumbria Police Headquarters control desk in pre-computer days.

room. Control was a rather basic affair then with a VHF radio for contacting mobile police officers, an ancient plug-in telephone switchboard and a very slow teleprinter machine. It took only two of us to run the place on nights – one sergeant and a constable. The workload could vary considerably between being quite hectic at times and virtually nothing at all at others.

The run of arrests during my first year on traffic patrol seemed to continue even when I was confined to the Control Room. Largely of course it was a case of being in the right place at the right time, and also I was never all that keen to report relatively minor breaches of the law, which perhaps left more time to look out for the more serious offences for which arrests could be made without warrant. This is not to imply any criticism of those of my colleagues who tended to report far more speeders, double white liners and so on than I did, because of course it would not have been right for people to think the police did not take such offences seriously. Anyway, it seemed to work for me even if this predilection for quality rather than quantity often put me at the bottom of the 'score-sheet' (the tally of arrests made and offences reported by patrol staff).

One night I reported for Control Room duty at the normal time of 9.45pm. The shift started in the usual way – update and general chat with the 2pm to 10pm shift just finishing, reading the day's message file, acknowledging mobile officers booking on and off and so on. Soon after 10pm the night sergeant and I had the place to ourselves.

Around 11pm things started to happen in a big way. A teenage girl had been stabbed with a knife in the town about a mile away and a local youth was strongly suspected of the attack. A large-scale search of the area got under way and there was much activity on our radio system. A description of the youth was sent to us in the control room for circulation throughout the force area.

I passed the description out on the telephone and on the radio many times over the next hour or so and it became imprinted in my memory. In particular, the most noticeable feature of the suspect's clothing was said to be a brightly coloured Fair Isle pullover.

The injured girl was reported to be in a serious condition. We were aware of the intensifying search for the youth going on in the area, and our control room became the focal point for several very senior officers who had been informed at home of what was happening (and were now serving no useful purpose whatsoever by standing around in the control room).

By about 1am the hunt seemed to be going a bit cold (like the aforementioned very senior officers who by now were going off to their beds). The two-man crew of the area traffic car came into the control room as usual at that time of night, for their refreshments. At this point the town police station came on the telephone to ask for loan of the powerful handlamps that were kept at force headquarters in the traffic patrol white Land Rover incident vehicle (the White Elephant mentioned earlier). Being familiar with the vehicle and its equipment, I offered to take the Land Rover down into the town and deliver the handlamps for the locals. The sergeant agreed to this and said he knew the suspect, adding that he was dangerous, so dangerous in fact that he thought he would 'knife a policeman before the night was out.'

In a show of mock bravado I said I would lock the youth up myself as well as taking the Land Rover to Penrith. One of the traffic car crew who was just starting on his sandwiches joined in the banter by offering me his truncheon. I did not have mine with me (why would I need one in the control room?), so I kept up the show of bravado by taking the proffered instrument and ostentatiously putting it into the uniform deep trouser pocket provided for holding these things. The sergeant was a jocular man who was very easy to get on with – with eight-hour night shifts confined to the control room it was just as well he was – and as I left the control room he shouted after me in jest, 'You've got twenty minutes to lock him up and get back here'.

'Right', I replied, heading off into the darkness to get the Land Rover out of the garage. I jumped in the vehicle and started for the town police station. In my haste, though, I had set off without checking that the lighting equipment was in the back. I had gone about half a mile down the road towards the town when I thought to look over my shoulder and realised I was short of the very things I was supposed to be delivering. It occurred to me that the handlamps which were normally left in this vehicle had probably been taken out for battery charging.

Cursing, I turned the Land Rover round and had just started to retrace my steps when the vehicle's headlights picked out a lone figure walking along the country road towards me. It was a youth wearing a Fair Isle pullover! The distinctive colours stood out from under his open jacket.

My friend the control room sergeant's prophecy of doom about the lad stabbing a policeman before the night was out rang in my ears as I pondered momentarily what to do for the best. I was on my own and it was pitch black. I decided not to use the vehicle radio handset or make any sudden movement because I thought either the lad would run away (leaving the search back where it started) or he might try and use his knife on me.

As I looked at the lad, I felt sure he was the youth everyone had been searching for these past two hours. Rightly or wrongly, I decided to feign ignorance – no talk of any stabbing or of arrest and no use of the radio. Instead I assumed a casual approach and asked the lad if he was going far. He replied, 'Just into Penrith.' I said, 'Well, jump in and I'll give you a lift. I'm going that way myself.' The lad got in the passenger seat beside me. He seemed docile enough, but with my hands on the steering wheel I felt very vulnerable. I wondered for a moment if I had done the right thing. In fact I was scared for my life. Anyway, I was committed now.

I set off into town without hurrying, making casual conversation with the lad about the weather and so on. He said he was walking home from a dance in the country but I was convinced I had the right man. I kept up the casual conversation as we drove through the town in the direction of the home address he had given me. This would take us past the police station as well, and I said I had a call to make there but would not be more than a minute or two.

When I got within a few yards of the police station front door, I thought, 'This is it!' I swung the wheel over hard left, bouncing the Land Rover up across the pavement, slammed on the brakes and leapt out. Back on my feet with the borrowed truncheon in my hand, my confidence was restored. I told the youth to get himself into the police station and quick. He did as he was told and I followed right behind him.

I directed the youth into the station control room and found the force detective superintendent and the local detective sergeant just in the process of drafting an express message about the incident for circulation to surrounding police forces. Their reaction to my entry, completely unannounced of course, was one of utter astonishment. Blasé as ever, I said simply, 'Mr Z for you' (he had a long surname).

Nobody spoke. Then the detective sergeant grabbed my new found friend by the arm and disappeared up the police station stairs with him to the CID office. Not a word to me. I was left standing there.

I got back in the trusty Land Rover and drove back the mile or so to police headquarters. As I went into the control room, I adopted a serious expression and told the sergeant I was sorry it had taken me rather more than the specified 20 minutes to get the job done and return to my post. Solemnly also, I gave the truncheon back with thanks to its owner, who was by now just finishing his refreshments. I was ready for a cup of tea myself.

Later that same night I accompanied the detective sergeant and the youth, who by now was officially under arrest for the attack on the girl, back to the spot on the road where I had first seen him. The lad led us into a field beside the road where we recovered a nasty looking dagger. It seemed the youth had thrown it over the roadside wall into the field when he saw me stop. I felt a bit thoughtful about that.

Next day I learned that the detective sergeant had been credited with making the arrest for attempted murder. I was simply required to make out a short statement. Nobody even thanked me. I learned a bit more about the police force that night and about the tendencies of at least one of its more ambitious members. The point was of course that the youth I took to the police station had been circulated in connection with the knife attack but I had not actually told him he had been arrested – not in so many words anyway – although obviously he must have known he was under arrest as soon as he went through the police station door. While I can't remember the sentence this lad got for this Cumbrian knife attack, he was eventually sentenced to life imprisonment for murder after a violent attack in Lancashire in which the victim's body was bundled down a manhole.

The old motor cycle continued to bring me the most success at this time in terms of arrests made. One incident, shortly after the knife affair just mentioned, also allowed me to make use of my new found sensitivity to the principle of taking credit for what you had done, without letting anybody else get in on it.

One fine evening I was travelling west on a routine motorcycle trip through the Lake District when I heard a message on my radio about a nasty attack on a woman in a small town about 20 miles away. In fact the incident was being circulated as one of attempted murder. A brief description of the wanted man was given along with details of a car he was believed to be driving. The brief radio message ended before I had had time to get the bike stopped and dig out a pencil and paper to write any of it down, but I did make a mental note of the details of the vehicle.

There was a bit of traffic about at the time, and several cars had just passed me travelling in the opposite direction. By the time I had taken in the radio message and particularly

Head on 'fatal' on the A6 road just before M6 opened in 1968.

digested details of the vehicle involved, the line of cars had gone out of sight. However, I had a feeling that one of these cars might have matched the description of the suspect's vehicle. I had no reason to think the car would be coming towards me because the incident had happened some distance away, but there was something about one of those cars I had just seen that had attracted my attention, even though it had gone before the radio message was finished.

I stopped at the roadside. After wondering for a moment if it was worthwhile, I decided to go and see if I could find the car concerned. This of course was where the manoeuvrability of the motorcycle was shown to advantage – no need to look for a road junction to turn round or even a gateway – just whip round in the road. After travelling briskly for a couple of miles or so I got the line of cars in my view. Having overtaken the last two or three, I came up behind the car I had been thinking about and got a look at the registration number. It was the wanted car! The driver was male but there appeared to be two or three young women passengers as well, which seemed surprising in the circumstances, but circumstances, but I was sure I had the right car.

There was nowhere to stop the car just then and in any case I was in hilly country where I suspected my radio would not work very well. After another mile or so I reached a hill crest where I got an immediate acknowledgement from control so I told them the situation and said I would be stopping the car on a pub car park a short distance ahead. The advantage of that of course was not only that there was room to stop the vehicle off the road but also there would no doubt be other people about who might help if things got troublesome. As I said, my information was simply that the car driver was suspected of attempted murder.

I overtook the car and attracted the attention of the driver, who followed me onto the pub car park and stopped. Going back to the car, I noticed the driver had some nasty looking scratches on his face, and a couple a questions convinced me he was the wanted man. I told him I was arresting him on suspicion of attempted murder and ordered him to stay where he was. I took the car's ignition key from the switch and confirmed the situation on the radio with control.

There were two young – and now very shaken – women hitchhikers in the car, whom our 'attempted murderer' had picked up after the attack on the injured woman. It seemed in my experience at this time to be not unusual for a man who had committed some serious offence, and who was afterwards driving a vehicle, to pick up a hitch-hiker or two, maybe as some sort of a diversionary tactic.

However, within a few minutes police assistance arrived on the pub car park in the shape of the local CID car. And who should jump out first but the detective sergeant who had just recently 'robbed' me of the glamour of an arrest for an apparently similar offence to the one we were dealing with here? While I might have credited him with a bit more subtlety, his first words to me were, 'Have you told him he is under arrest?' Not going to be caught out again so easily, I looked him in the eye and said emphatically, 'Yes, I have.' He looked disappointed.

My detainee in this case turned out to be a local businessman who had a number of restaurants in the area. Each establishment was run by a manageress and that day he had been travelling round them all picking up the week's cash takings. He had apparently fallen out in a big way with one of the ladies and she ended up in hospital. By the time I stopped him he had over £2,000 cash about his person, which was a lot of money then. (My gross pay at the time was £69 per month for round-the-clock shifts).

It was surprising what you could see – or sometimes perhaps sense – when you were just standing at the side of a busy main road, particularly if the traffic was heavy and slow moving. The advantage of the motorcycle of course was the ability to set off from the roadside quickly in either direction without any manoeuvring about and regardless of traffic conditions. Unlike a car, you were never hemmed in by other traffic. As a police motorcyclist, you had a feeling of being in charge of the traffic, rather than just stuck in it as you would be in a car.

One day I was stationary by the side of the A6 trunk road with the motorcycle. I was not doing much on the face of it but was watching the passing traffic and had stolen car numbers and so on in the back of my mind. Most drivers would glance your way as they passed, if traffic was not moving too quickly. One van driver on this occasion just stared straight ahead. It was a large van and he had a couple of young women in the cab with him.

Deciding to follow the van as it disappeared off south and coming up behind it a mile or so away, I thought somehow the driver did not seem too comfortable. He didn't appear to be travelling with the usual confidence and steadiness of the professional driver who would have been expected to be in charge of this kind of large vehicle.

I moved in front of the van and motioned to the driver to stop on a lay-by. As usual, I was watching the vehicle very carefully as it slowed down, to make sure it was not going to ram me from behind, particularly when I was in the vulnerable situation of having brought the bike to a stop but not yet having got off it. (It was not unknown for a heavy goods vehicle to hit the back of a police vehicle that was bringing it to a stop and then for the HGV driver to claim that the driver of the badly shortened police car had not given him room to pull up).

However, the new-found friend in this case got stopped all right. At first he claimed to be in legitimate possession of the van but could not produce any documents. When I said I was going to have my control get in touch with the vehicle's owners, he admitted he had stolen it in Scotland. The two girls with him turned out to be hitch-hikers who had no idea they were travelling in a stolen vehicle.

I got a police car to take the van driver and his two innocent passengers into town while I followed on the motor cycle. Later that day I got a lift back to where the van had been left and drove it to the police station also. It was a cumbersome thing that was not in good order and I could see why the man I had collared had not seemed too happy with it, quite apart from any discomfort he might have felt about being followed closely by a police bike. I was glad I was only driving the van a few miles.

I had quite a bit of success that first year or so on main road motorcycle patrol. By success I mean in the sense of making arrests without warrant, which was obviously the most interesting and rewarding part of the job. I put it down to a combination of factors. Naturally, you needed a bit of luck in the sense of being in the right place at the right time.

HEADQUARTERS TRAFFIC PATROL

Traffic police preparing for M6 opening in 1968.

But I was already a fairly experienced motorcyclist who could devote a lot of attention to being a policeman rather than just controlling the bike. And I was always keen to be out on the road as much as possible, without spending too much time in the office doing reports about relatively minor traffic offences.

At the end of this first year on traffic patrol I was suddenly called up to the chief constable's office. It was with some trepidation that I reported to the great man's presence but I need not have worried. The chief said he saw a lot of paper on his desk but he had not overlooked what he had seen about the successes I had been having with incidents coming my way. With just three years' police service at this time, I was naturally very pleased that I had come to the favourable attention of the chief constable for practical police work.

The superintendent in charge of the traffic department – a rather detached sort of individual who often seemed to get people's names wrong – was less enthusiastic. In fact I did not think he was particularly interested.

Maybe I was still a bit naive. I had tended to play down the successes I had been having because I simply thought a policeman should take things in his stride without making too much noise about it, and I instinctively had the most regard for policemen who did not blow their own trumpets too much. I had yet to learn that so often in the police it was not so much a question of what you did but rather of what you said you did. It seemed surprising that policemen who would claim to spot deviousness in the public could sometimes be blind to the conmen in their own ranks. In this case Chief Constable Frank Williamson had noticed my activities while the people between him and me at my humble level were less interested. I had been congratulated by the chief but there was nothing on paper about it in the way of an official commendation so there was no permanent record. When the chief left Cumbria a year or so later his expression of appreciation to me went with him.

Incidentally, Chief Constable Williamson was reputed to have a remarkable memory for detail, including the ability to recall the name of every member of the local force. One night I was at the scene of a very nasty road accident in which a police colleague was killed when Mr Williamson himself appeared out of the darkness and said, 'Everything under control, Sharpe?' Though astonished that the chief constable should have turned out in person, even to so tragic an occurrence as the accidental death of a policeman (and surprised that he knew my name), I quickly recovered my composure and assured him all was in order.

Mr Williamson left Cumbria soon afterwards to become a member of HM Inspectorate of Constabulary. In that capacity he was appointed to lead an inquiry into much-publicised allegations of corruption involving senior CID officers of the Metropolitan Police. Doubtless he approached the job with his customary punctiliousness and energy but eventually he admitted defeat and resigned his post on the grounds that he did not get the co-operation he deserved from the capital's police. Despite his personal qualities of integrity and and sobriety, perhaps he was not the right man for that particular job. 'Horses for courses…'

Naturally, however, traffic patrol in the main was not about the 'glamour' bits like making arrests but far more about being conspicuous and preventing trouble happening (while at the same time perhaps hoping it would). There were always the abnormal loads to look after, accidents to deal with and checks to do on road-users (on wheels or on foot) who attracted your attention as possible villains on the move.

Despite the vast increase in traffic volume in recent years, it is a fact that around four times as many people died in road accidents in the 1960s than fifty years later. Dealing with a serious accident was always a challenge but hardly the traumatic business it is sometimes made out to be these days. Certainly no accident I dealt with ever left me distressed to the extent of needing counselling or whatever. This is not,I hope, to appear insensitive because an accident is terribly unpleasant for those unfortunate enough to be directly involved. The point is that it is all part of the job and if you, as a policeman, can't handle it with equanimity, then who can? You rise to the occasion because people expect you to – and you have your own self-esteem to think about as well.

The best way to deal with any road accident was to put things in a logical sequence according to priorities. It was as well to remember that rushing to the scene could sometimes be spectacularly counter-productive. However serious the occurrence, the odd minute or so saved by racing there with two-tone horns blaring and lights flashing was hardly going to make much difference. The main thing was to get there safely and arrive calmly with some sort of plan about what you were going to do.

I always remember setting off in a four-wheeled police vehicle to the scene of a serious road accident involving a heavy goods vehicle in conditions that were said to be icy. The road surface did not seem slippery to me on the way there but as usual my instinct was to take it steady. As I rounded a slight bend on the main road not far short of the accident scene I came upon the ambulance that had been on its way to the same incident. It was upside down in the road and the crew were just scrambling out. They were shaken but unhurt, and I ended up dealing with their accident. None of us was of any use to the unfortunate driver who died under his lorry less than a mile away.

So the first thing in dealing with a road accident was to get there – without fail. Having arrived, the first thing was to protect the scene. It would he hopeless to have someone else crash into the wreckage. Obviously that meant using any warning signs at your disposal and also getting people to go down the road and flag down approaching traffic. Then put your own vehicle, if possible, between the scene and the approaching traffic.

After these vital preliminaries the next thing was to assess the situation more closely. Anyone injured? Ambulance called? Even if it has been, use your wireless and check giving the control room an initial assessment. I found there was rarely much need for practising first aid at road accidents. Usually, the best thing to do was very little in that respect until the ambulance arrived. Sometimes of course the ambulance got there before you did – barring the unusual case related above! Otherwise, it was not far behind.

Preserving the evidence was the next priority (occasionally even preserving the peace, because drivers who have suddenly come in contact with each other can get very nasty about it). Any independent witnesses? Get their names and addresses with a view to seeing them later. Make any appropriate measurements with the vehicles still in situ – but if they have to be moved then mark their positions. If it is a fatal accident or seems likely to become one, then get the police photographer.

Getting the road cleared was next. In my day, this was treated as a high priority, but nowadays roads often seem to stay closed for a long time after serious accidents. Police these days can bring to bear a lot of specialist expertise in investigating road accidents, but long delays in such cases sometimes give rise to the feeling that once the road is closed it can stay closed purely for the convenience of people at the scene and without any regard for the interests of other road users. Prolonged frustration in such cases can have serious consequences.

Anyway, having got the road cleared and taken all your notes and measurements and so on at the scene, your main problems were often just starting – the paperwork, the bit that generally nobody sees. To get the file together for an injury accident would probably take several hours. If there had been a fatality then it could well be days or even weeks before you would get it finalised. Eventually the matter might end up in court or at an inquest and perhaps resurrect itself as a civil case a year or two afterwards.

Enough of the technicalities, however. Six shining new BSA 'Police Special' patrol motorcycles had been delivered to the dealers in the town, where they were being made ready for the road. They were the very latest thing, all white with blue light on the front and the 'D' registration. I was lucky enough to get one, even though I was probably one of the junior members of the department in terms of police service, and my old machine that had served me so well was then pensioned off.

For some reason I never did seem to have the same success on the road with the nice new bike that I had had with the old black one. Maybe it was just too conspicuous – and it certainly had to be looked after better. I remember one hot day having to follow a car along a newly surfaced stretch of road and then being obliged to spend ages with tar remover cleaning up the white front of the bike that was plastered with the stuff.

Actually, the amount of time I was spending on the bike at this time was rather tailing off as I was required to use four wheels more often. It was seen officially as some sort of progression from two wheels to four but I was never entirely convinced. Obviously the car was more comfortable but you did feel more isolated from people than on a bike and moreover you were often just stuck in traffic like everyone else.

By this time we had radar speed detectors, and it fell to my lot to operate one of these things more frequently than I would have liked. We always gave a generous allowance over the speed limit (usually ten miles per hour at least), but I was never happy about using the radar because it felt a bit underhand and I thought I might be missing something more interesting while I was focussing all my attention on speeders and doing the subsequent paperwork. These radar machines were never 100% reliable, although they did 'fail safe' in the sense that they would not over-read and would simply stop functioning if a fault developed. (Secretly I was always pleased if the thing did conk out and then I could fetch it in and get on with something more interesting).

Reporting speeding drivers en masse like this always left

Police car on the new M6 in Cumbria.

me feeling a bit uneasy. I could not help thinking that our job should be about prevention, not detection, preferably by being as conspicuous as possible. Actually, reporting speeding offences with the motor cycle was a rarity for me and was usually confined to the more blatant cases such as when drivers overtook me when I was already travelling at the relevant speed limit. That did happen now and again. In such cases the excuses of the drivers concerned could be quite interesting. For example:-

a) Scots lorry driver on a level road approaching a hill: 'Keeping ma revs up for the brae, Jimmy.'

b) Another Scots lorry driver: 'Aye, but where's your mate, Jimmy?' (overlooking the fact that Scottish law on corroboration did not apply south of the border).

c) Furniture van driver: 'Forty miles an hour speed limit with this thing? Nobody in the office told me about that.'

Lest anyone should suspect me of racial bias, I hasten to say we were less than thirty miles south of the Scottish border and a large proportion of our main road traffic was travelling to and from the Glasgow area. Then again, our local drivers could be very short-sighted, in more ways than one. I recall remonstrating with a Cumbrian farmer who gave me quite a shock on the motorcycle by driving his tractor and muck-spreader past a 'Give-Way' sign, out of a side road and right across my bows. He let me finish my little lecture and then said quietly, 'Aye, well lad, Ah've driven out of there like that for t'last thirty year and Ah's gonna continue to do so as long as thoo's nut watching me!'

I knew the sun was definitely setting on my career as a main-road motor cyclist when they sent me on a patrol car driving course. It was a local 'Standard B' affair of three weeks' duration and the next best thing to the full month's advanced course for which we Cumbrians had to go to Lancashire. The sergeant instructor was a very polished driver himself and indeed something of a perfectionist who could express himself forcibly on the driving weaknesses of those in his charge. Mine was only his second such course and he probably had a right to be a bit tense.

Relaxing on his course was out, even if you were one of the two pupils sitting in the back of the car awaiting your turn for the hot seat. He had a habit of suddenly whipping round in his front seat as you were going along and snapping at somebody in the back a question about the last road sign, or whatever, that we had just passed. Without suggesting our leader was totally devoid of a sense of humour, he was definitely not amused when a rear seat passenger (not me) answered one of these snap questions with 'King's Arms, sergeant.'

By this time also we had a new man in charge of the Traffic Department, a gentleman who came to us from a Midlands force on promotion and was not quite what we taciturn northerners were used to. Chief super Ron was a remarkable character who proved to be one of those rarities in the police force – a man still talked about long after he had retired. An ex-Navy man and something of a legend in his own life time, you could not possibly be indifferent to him. Contemptuous as he was of any signs of complacency among his staff, his style was attack, and any hint of weakness in the face of such attack sent him straight for the jugular (figuratively speaking of course).

I recall him once 'getting a grip' of me for a minor administrative error that could not possibly have been mine because I had been on leave at the time. Never one to take such things lying down (or perhaps simply foolhardy), I assembled my evidence of innocence in the matter and went back to tell him that as far as I was concerned I had just received an unjustified reprimand. Unabashed, chief super Ron snapped back: 'Yes, well, unjustified reprimands are issued in the interests of efficiency!' And he meant it, because that seemed to be part of his professional philosophy.

That said however, it was my good fortune to get on well with the chief super. By this time construction was starting in Cumbria of about 70 miles of the M6 motorway through the county from north to south, bypassing the old A6 bottlenecks like Carlisle, Penrith and Kendal and also the then notorious road over Shap Fell. Serious traffic disruption was inevitable while the work went on and I was assigned to a traffic management role.

The new motorway with its implications for the police was the chief superintendent's pet subject at this time and I had the distinction of being his right hand man in that particular sphere. What it amounted to was regular liaison with contractors, surveyors, highway authorities and so on to try and minimise danger and disruption to normal road traffic. In the later stages, as sections of the new motorway opened to the public, I had to prepare the appropriate operation orders for diverting traffic from the old roads on to the motorway. Finally, it became my responsibility to develop and publish guidance to police patrols on motorway law and procedure.

All this motorway mania came to a conclusion with completion of construction early in 1971, when I crowned my involvement in it with the privilege of being the first to drive over the 30-mile M6 section bypassing Kendal and Shap Fell, after the tape was ceremonially cut by the Minister of Transport. (I was the driver of the police escort vehicle leading a convoy of a dozen cars and buses carrying dignitaries associated with the project).

After gaining a class 1 certificate on the Lancashire Constabulary advanced driving course, I was confined to control room duty for about six months (logical no doubt) before returning to traffic car patrol. No doubt it was reasonable that I should do a spell of control room duty at this time because the control was a new one that had been planned for opening with the motorway and I had been involved with planning certain aspects of it that were directly concerned with the motorway. For example, all the blue emergency telephone boxes at one-mile intervals along the motorway terminated at consoles in the force control room and all such calls had to be treated initially as a police matter, even though about 95% turned out to be vehicle breakdowns that were simply passed on to the appropriate agency. Hapless callers' unfamiliarity with the motorway telephone system was often surprising:-

'Sorry to bother you but I've walked miles along the motorway and I just can't find a yellow phone box.

They're all blue.'

'What do you mean?'

'Well, I'm in the AA.' Or –

'Polis? Polis? Och, no, Ah dinna want the polis! Ah've broken doon.' (Phone went dead).

Early in March 1972 I was sitting in a patrol car on the motorway somewhere south of Penrith when I got a radio call to return to headquarters at once. I headed north briskly and had got about half way there when there was another call demanding to know where I was. I gave my location and really put my foot to the floor thinking it must be something serious. When I arrived at the front door of the headquarters building a few minutes later I was met by the chief superintendent himself. He did not tell me what it was all about but just bundled me up the stairs into the chief constable's office. He looked pleased so I concluded it could not be trouble.

4
STAFF OFFICER

The Chief Constable was a dauntingly haughty-looking individual whose origins far from Cumbria were detectable in a West Country burr that the amateur impressionists among us were fond of imitating – from a safe distance behind his back, of course. By the mid-1960s he had been Chief Constable of Brighton, a small borough force which lost its separate identity in the police amalgamations of the later 60s, and he had then come north to replace our previous chief who left to become an Inspector of Constabulary.

My path had first crossed the chief's a little while earlier when I acted for a few weeks as his official driver while his regular man was in hospital. He had already established himself in Cumbria as not a man to be crossed – and one or two had the scars to prove it – but personally I had had nothing but courtesy from him. A very tall man who looked a bit like the late lamented Christopher Lee in Count Dracula mode with maybe a dash of comedian Bruce Forsyth about him as well, he had an air of authority that bordered on the imperious, and yet anyone with the courage to look him in the eye would have detected an occasional twinkle that suggested he was not taking himself too seriously after all. As an authoritarian figure in a hierarchical organisation, he was bound to attract his share of sycophants, but there was little doubt about his ability to distinguish genuine respect from mere obsequiousness.

While he had the theatrical flair to assume an air of pomposity if the occasion seemed to him to justify it, he was dismissive of anyone less polished in that respect than he was. He told me one day of a meeting he had attended with a counterpart from a large northern police force who was destined for notoriety over his reported claims to divine connections. In the space of an hour of so this worthy had apparently distinguished himself by using the word dichotomy no less than nine times. 'Nine times,' the chief recalled, 'I counted them.' It seemed to be the in-word in the higher echelons of the service at that particular time.

As something of a legendary figure, it was not always easy to distinguish fact from fiction in the stories that circulated about him. However, he was genuinely proud of the police service and concerned to guard its independence against people he regarded as nosey-parkers. He was especially suspicious of the media, and press people with the temerity to approach him for information on police matters would probably be sent his standard letter, setting out what amounted to a policy of co-operation on his terms only and ending with an emphatic 'and that is my policy and I do not intend to alter it to accommodate you.' In similar vein, a member of the teaching profession asked him (probably with rather less deference than he was accustomed to): 'Tell me, what is a chief constable's function? What do you actually do?' The chief looked out of the window and replied, 'Bagger all.'

He was no admirer of the Police Federation (the police 'union') or of the trade union influences that were starting to appear in the job at this time as police civilian staff were tending to increase in number. A police garage storeman, who had been elected shop steward, told me about going to see the chief once on a union matter and being rebuffed with the statement that, 'If you have time to involve yourself in this sort of thing then I can only conclude that you are not fully employed and your services will be dispensed with.' Needless to say, the union man did not bother him again.

The chief constable certainly had an eye for the ladies.

Hardly a particularly religious man, his presence in church was once remarked on by someone whose inquisitiveness was rewarded with the information that, 'Yes, but where else would you see so many ladies on their own?' As a sprightly sexagenarian with limited opportunity to join young lady members of his staff on the dance floor, he was once moved to ask a rather reluctant dance partner with well known equine interests, 'Miss McInnes, why are you holding me on a loose rein?'

The chief was often to be seen with a glass in his hand, his favourite tipple being a gin and tonic – although it was as well to be as prudent as usual in talking to him when he had a glass in his hand because you could never be sure whether the contents were all gin or all tonic. But he certainly believed in the value of *in vino veritas*. A superintendent post had become vacant and been advertised nationally as these things sometimes were. The due processes had produced a short list of about six who had come to force HQ for interview. The chief took aside the chief superintendent who would have to work with the new man, whoever he turned out to be, and counselled him about his approach to the applicants on the following lines:

'Take them down to the George Hotel. Ply them with drink. Some will be verbose, others will be lachrymose and one or two may be comatose, and you will find the man you want.'

Though not a public school product himself, the chief had perfected the public school habit of calling people by their surnames, and he never deviated from that. Even his deputy was always addressed and referred to by his surname. This was entirely consistent with the chief's autocratic demeanour, although again in this there was sometimes just a hint of his capacity not to take it all too seriously. Just after an official visit to Cumbria by HRH Prince Charles, during which the Prince's list of engagements had included a call at police HQ, the chief was in self-congratulatory mood as he reflected on the occasion, glass in hand. Drawing himself up to his full 6'3' or so, he confided in me as to how he had got the Prince to include us in his itinerary: 'Windsor,' I said, 'Windsor, you must come and see my police headquarters, and he did.' You could almost imagine him doing that (and maybe he did for all I know).

Anyway, I digress – the chief looked at me over his glasses from behind his desk as I entered his inner sanctum and said, 'Sharpe, I'm going to promote you. I'm making you a sergeant. You'll have a staff officer function but we can't really call it that at present. You'll be in administration.'

The local force had grown rather bigger recently, and the authorised establishment now included an assistant chief constable in addition to the chief and his deputy. One outcome of this was that the deputy chief constable and assistant chief constable were to have a shared secretary (the chief already had his own), and the triumvirate (if you could really call it that with an autocratic chief like this one) was going to have the services of a staff officer – me. I had had not an inkling of this, which was unusual in a rumour-rife job like ours, and no idea what the task would involve. As usual, I would just have to find out for myself, although the chief did emphasise one thing in particular: 'The assistant chief constable is new here. He does not know his way round. I want you to look after him.' I took careful note of that.

I was not in the Presence long. My next call was on the chief superintendent (administration/staff planning). He dealt with a few formalities without saying much more than he really had to, although he did allow himself a comment to the effect that it was marvellous what a trip to London with the chief could do for you (referring presumably to a recent journey to the capital that I had done as the chief constable's temporary driver).

Taking that as the best I was going to get from him by way of congratulation, I countered by suggesting that I supposed we were always on interview. The normal system was that this chief superintendent and the deputy chief constable got together to decide whose names were going forward to the chief for promotion, and I heard subsequently that they had had someone else in mind for this particular post of staff officer. In this case, however, the chief had apparently made his own decision so, through no fault of my own, I was seen as having 'bucked the system' – a slight initial obstacle to overcome.

Aged only 40-ish, the deputy chief constable was a shrewd and tight-lipped Cumbrian whose recent promotions had come in rapid succession, and he had taken on his present post only a matter of weeks earlier when his predecessor had died suddenly in office. He was said to be difficult to work for because of a short temper – not a good thing in a policeman – and an inability to communicate what he wanted, although personally I did not find any real problems in that respect. The deputy chief constable of a police force has a personal responsibility for disciplinary matters and complaints from the public, and it was in this particular sphere that I was to find I had far more dealings with the deputy chief constable than with the chief constable or the assistant chief constable. New as he was to the job, the deputy chief constable clearly did not want a 'yes' man as his assistant who would simply agree with everything he said, even though conformity is the general rule in the police service.

In fact, after a short period of initial reserve from the deputy chief constable, probably arising from the circumstances of my appointment to the staff officer job as already mentioned, I came to have a high regard for him. The alleged problems of working for him, which caused a lot of others to grimace, did not materalise in my case because of my quickly-found facility for anticipating what he would want in most circumstances without bothering him with a lot of questions beforehand. The 'I don't want questions, I just want answers' approach suited me fine. In his position I would have expected no less myself.

The new assistant chief constable was a different sort of man altogether – also quite young for the post but a smooth talker and perhaps a bit of a showman. He looked rather like actor Roger Moore, and he said himself that he was more likely to be taken for a bank manager than a policeman. I soon struck up a good working relationship with him, particularly in the matter of looking after internal force promotion boards which he chaired by reason of his office.

Quite understandably, the new man soon wanted to know a bit about those in the organization he would be having the most dealings with, so I gave him a quick outline of a few people. Thinking, however, that the assistant chief constable might want to be something of an individualist, and bearing in mind the chief constable's recent instruction to me that I was to look after the new man, I was in no doubt that the best way I could carry out my brief in that respect was to advise the assistant chief constable to be cautious in his dealings with the gentleman who had given me the instruction. The assistant chief constable listened to the short counsel – no names mentioned but a finger pointed towards the chief's office next door – and said, 'Yes, John, but he won't break me.' Well, time would tell.

My first task of any consequence in the staff officer role was set by the chief constable himself. It was early 1972, and in Cumbria we were soon to take over from Lancashire responsibility for policing the Furness District of that county, together with a small part of West Yorkshire (or the West Riding of Yorkshire as it was known then). This was to coincide with the major re-organisation of local government boundaries that would remove from the map old-established county names like Westmorland.

Furness at this time formed a division of the Lancashire Constabulary, and the impending effect of its incorporation into Cumbria would be to increase the size of our force from three territorial divisions to four, while the small Yorkshire addition would be relatively insignificant. Planning was getting under way for the changes but little was known throughout the force generally about what was happening in this respect. The chief constable decided to circulate a bulletin outlining the proposed changes, and he told me to prepare something suitable. I drafted out a summary of my rather limited understanding of the situation and laced the text with a few maps and diagrams. The draft was approved and the thing was duly given wide circulation throughout the force. It only amounted to a few pages but it looked quite nice and I was rather proud of my handiwork. I reasoned that more than a few pages would be boring, and in any case I doubted if I knew enough myself to write any more on the subject.

Anyway, my handiwork must have suited the chief, who observed with obvious satisfaction that I had 'written four pages and told them nothing.' Having established my credentials by passing this test, I was to find that a major part of my new role at force headquarters was to develop a facility for committing to paper material which left the reader feeling as comfortable as possible without actually telling him anything that mattered. Anyone who can steel himself to listen carefully to politicians' turgid pronouncements will know what I mean. The fundamental objective of course was to use words not so much to impart information as to create an atmosphere of affability and concern in which you are unlikely to be troubled with that particular problem again.

Nowhere was the search for the *mot juste* more important than in dealing with public complaints against the police. Allegations of misconduct by policemen were not particularly common at this time (perhaps one or two a week on average in Cumbria), and the law on the subject was set out in only one section of the Police Act 1960, which said in effect that complaints were to be recorded promptly and investigated. Apart from a requirement for the county Police Authority to keep itself informed about the way these matters were dealt with and an annual check by the office of HM Inspector of Constabulary, the procedure was very much a matter for the deputy chief constable of the police force concerned.

In essence, any complaint from a member of the public alleging that a police officer had committed a disciplinary or criminal offence was brought to the attention of the deputy chief constable. If he decided it amounted to a complaint under section 49 of the Police Act, then brief details were entered in the HQ Complaints Book and it was acknowledged briefly by letter from the deputy chief constable to the complainant (or to the individual bringing the matter to attention on his behalf such as a solicitor or Member of Parliament). Although this reply was invariably only a non-committal couple of sentences, its composition was best treated carefully because it was the first indication the complainant would get that his problem had reached a very senior level in the police. Apart from any question of public relations, a decent letter of acknowledgement in the hands of the complainant, whatever his background or status, was likely to make the investigating officer's job a little bit easier.

The main thing with this letter was never to treat it as a

stereotype but always to try to relate it to your initial assessment of the complainant and of the circumstances. Obviously a regular complainant against police or an individual with a long list of criminal convictions to his credit was not going to merit a lot of attention, but the basic principle of courtesy always applied. However hostile, aggressive or unpleasant the terms of the complaint – and some solicitors in particular could write some surprisingly aggressive letters for their clients – the acknowledgement was always courteous and to the point.

Having got the complaint recorded and acknowledged, the next step was to appoint an investigating officer – usually a superintendent. At this time in Cumbria there were not a lot of superintendents to choose from. Complaint inquiries were additional to their normal responsibilities, and you could imagine their feelings when getting the ominous-looking buff envelope from force HQ. But what normally represented success in this particular area of policing was the eventual receipt at HQ of a brief report from the superintendent enclosing a signed statement by the complainant indicating his decision to withdraw his complaint or at least not to pursue it. That of course made things a lot easier for all concerned – including me with my responsibility for drafting the deputy chief constable's final letter to the complainant.

A decision by the complainant to pursue his allegations could lead to a time-consuming inquiry by the appointed officer and preparation of a substantial file requiring a decision on the question of possible criminal or disciplinary proceedings against the police officer(s) concerned. In practice, such proceedings were very rare. Many complaints against police could be regarded as little more than unfortunate misunderstandings between two individuals (one police officer and one member of the public) who had met suddenly in a potential conflict situation where the policeman thought he was just doing his job and the member of the public did not like the way he went about it. Some complaints of course were from people who had been arrested or reported for an offence and probably thought they could influence the police decision on proceedings if they went on the offensive with an allegation about the conduct of the policeman involved.

Occasionally, of course, complaints against police could appear so well-founded and potentially serious at the outset that there could be no question of adopting the 'play it down' or 'delay it' approach that may be detectable from some of my comments above. One such case in which I became involved, both as the HQ administrator of these matters and as an investigator, began with a strongly worded letter of protest from a Member of Parliament and a number of complaints from some very aggrieved parents of teenage boys.

A party of about a dozen youths between the ages of about fourteen and eighteen (and one or two perhaps slightly younger than that) had been travelling back from a day out in Blackpool to their homes in West Cumbria. They were all in an old van which broke down during the late evening, and the situation came to the attention of the local police. The repair was going to take some time, and all the boys were taken for shelter to the local police station, where they were allowed to sit and stand about in the public entrance hall. They became restless and rowdy and eventually a young policeman, tired of his efforts to control them, told them all to clear off. They left the police station and apparently set off to walk home. Unfortunately, it was now about midnight and their homes were 40 miles away.

Inevitably becoming split up, the boys straggled into their homes in groups of two or three throughout most of the following day. Some may have got lifts for at least part of the journey but others claimed to have walked the whole way.

Fortunately none of them appeared to suffer any lasting ill-effects but, looking on the black side, the possible consequences could have been disastrous and the police would obviously have borne a heavy responsibility for anything that befell them after they left the police station.

The complaints were duly recorded, and seeing all the people concerned took quite some time. The parents were generally decent working-class people, and certainly the ones I saw received me courteously into their homes in a rather run-down former mining area. It fell to my lot at the end of the inquiry to prepare the detailed covering report, but no less taxing of my literary skills was the problem of drafting about ten letters to the various parents, indicating that appropriate disciplinary action had been taken (without revealing what that was), each letter saying substantially the same thing but with slight variations in layout and wording to suggest individual attention in the event of comparisons being made by any of the recipients. Several months by now had elapsed since the affair began, but the thing ended there – no expressions of dissatisfaction with what had been done about all the complaints but, perhaps remarkably, one letter of appreciation from a parent about the way the matter had been handled. (That probably said a lot more about that individual's magnanimity than about any professionalism on our part, but it was nevertheless very much appreciated).

Public complaints and internal force discipline were inter-related matters under the direct responsibility of the deputy chief constable, and as staff officer I was closely involved in the administration of both. Disciplinary infringements deemed serious enough to be brought before the chief constable at a formal hearing at police headquarters were a comparative rarity and probably happened no more than once a year. The appointed day for such a hearing had very senior officers in uniforms they were not all that accustomed to, and everyone not directly involved 'keeping his head down', with a general effect probably not unlike the atmosphere prevailing in a prison establishment in the days when they had hangings. I could probably have counted on the fingers of one hand the times I arranged such a hearing during my five-year tenure of office at the Kremlin (as police HQ was sometimes known), but one of them particularly comes to mind.

A sergeant based at a police station some distance from police HQ had been charged with a disciplinary offence relating to the falsification of an entry in an official record (apparently intended to get a relative out of a driving offence). The usual formal notices to attend the hearing at 11am had gone out in good time to all concerned, including the accused officer, and by 10.45am there was a deathly hush on the top landing of police HQ. All office doors normally left open were firmly shut, fear of involvement in the proceedings overcoming even the nosiness for which the place was normally noted. The actual hearing was nothing to do with me, and I had my door closed also.

Suddenly my door burst open and in rushed big Dick, the superintendent who was to act as presenting officer (equivalent to prosecutor) at the hearing. Not normally a man to panic, Dick looked wild-eyed as he asked me, 'Have you seen Norman?' (the accused). 'Where the hell is he?'

Trying to keep calm in a crisis, I said I had not seen him. I knew I had sent out the appropriate notice and got an acknowledgement. Nothing like this had happened before in the history of the universe – it was like somebody being late for his own funeral.

I rang the police station where our accused man was based. I believe indeed his living quarters were above the station. After a few seconds the 'phone was answered by a sleepy voice which I immediately recognised as that of the absent defendant. What does one say in such circumstances? Rising to the occasion, however, I said quietly into the 'phone (not wishing to shock a man I had obviously just disturbed from deep slumber): 'Norman, haven't you forgotten something?'

Norman (after a pause) – 'I don't think so. Why?'

'Discipline hearing? Here at 11?' I ventured.

'Oh, hell,' was the reply. 'I had a late finish last night. I clean forgot.'

I suggested to the sergeant that he might start getting a move on. Big Dick had been listening to this brief conversation, and what little remained of his composure dissolved in a torrent of expletives. He shot off back along the corridor towards the chief's office, shouting, 'He'll go flipping crackers,' or words to that effect. I got the traffic department to give the sergeant a fast run to HQ but the damage was done. Despite the attempted arrogation to themselves of divine powers by one or two members of the HQ hierarchy and the impression the place created of being detached in a time-warp like a sort of less-than-benign Brigadoon, not even a directive from HQ could make the clock run backwards. The unfortunate sergeant met the chief an hour late, and his time in the police force ended there and then. Justice was dispensed (or dispensed with as the case may be). Even Big Dick was visibly shaken by it all.

If the tone of what I have said on the subject of discipline and complaints against police should seem rather flippant at times, then I would emphasize that it was something that needed careful handling and was always treated as confidential by all concerned. Dispassionate examination of many 'rubber heel jobs', as complaint enquiries tended to be called, would have suggested that in themselves they were not big issues, but they were always very important to those individuals directly involved. Certainly I never came across any case of a policeman treating a complaint lightly – quite the reverse in fact was the rule.

Be that as it may, the main consideration in dealing with the administration of such matters was to do everything possible to make it all look right on paper. The complainant was always going to get his two letters, one at each end of the affair, and whatever was written to him might well be subject also to critical examination by someone like his solicitor or Member of Parliament. As already noted, the Police Committee had to take an interest in these issues, and files were examined by the Inspector of Constabulary's staff at the annual inspection of the force. Unfortunately, the individual at risk of being given the least consideration in all this was often the police officer complained against, and his chances of redress in the event of a genuine grievance about it were effectively nil and not worth raising.

As far as I personally was aware, I had never had a 'Section 49' complaint recorded against me in my ten years' police service to date, and the air of mystery surrounding the whole subject was such that my knowledge of it at the outset was scant. With no disrespect to the deputy chief constable, his early familiarity with this very important part of his overall function was little greater than mine since he had inherited the task without prior notice from the previous deputy chief constable, who had died suddenly. This gentleman had been a policeman of the old school who had done things his own way, without too much regard for procedural niceties, and administration of complaints and matters of discipline was something he had kept very much to himself. However, this was now the 1970s and people were no longer accepting without question what the police did. Whether we liked it or not, we had to get used to playing it by the rules.

Another area that fell to my lot at this time had to be accorded at least as much secrecy as the subject of complaints and discipline. The new assistant chief constable assumed responsibility for force promotion boards and I had to do the necessary administration and safeguard the relevant records. The idea was that all sergeants and constables who were eligible for promotion (by examination and length of service) should be able to appear from time to time at headquarters before a board consisting of the assistant chief constable and two other senior officers with a view to being assessed as to their suitability in that respect.

The board members had before them a written divisional assessment of each officer who presented himself for his 20-minute interview, and their job was to grade him A, B or C (with the permitted slight variation of + or - in each case). The interviewee never knew what his division had said about him or what grading he was given by the board. Some comments could be quite remarkable. In the case of one hopeful sergeant, the assessment report of his divisional chief superintendent simply read, 'I despair that this man will ever mature' – and personally I could see the chief super's point, although the individual concerned somehow did eventually reach the rank of superintendent. In another case that comes to mind, an individualistic sort of constable had his assessment form endorsed by the board chairman after interview, 'An extraordinary fellow!' He reached the rank of inspector.

In view of all the secrecy and the fact that interviewees were not told their gradings, it was possible for candidates to be given a lower grading at one interview than they had got at their previous appearance before the board. I remember an acquaintance of mine (an ex-police cadet who really ought to have remained at the level of constable) being graded A+ at his first promotion board and something like B- at the second, which effectively put him out of the running (but was probably accurate in my view), and yet eventually he reached the rank of inspector.

In general, however, I thought the promotion board system, superficial though it may have been at first sight, worked out not too badly in practice. At least everyone from the divisions who was interested in his chances of advancement, whatever his own senior officers thought of him, had the chance to come and put his case at force headquarters. Where things could go wrong was above the level of the promotion board chairman (the assistant chief constable) who may have had the last word in setting the gradings but had nothing to do with making the actual promotions or even with putting forward the recommendations in that respect to the chief constable as promoting authority.

One memorable day I had to open up my securely locked cabinet of promotion board material in order to take up to the deputy chief constable's office my prepared list of sergeants graded A or A+ at their last promotion board. These were the only gradings that really counted and all names going forward to the chief constable for promotion to the rank of inspector were taken from this list. There were only about a dozen of them.

A vacancy for an inspector had arisen in one of the divisions, and it was the deputy chief constable's job in consultation with the chief superintendent (admin/staff planning) to make the appropriate recommendation to the chief constable. One or two other things of lesser importance were also being discussed in the deputy chief constable's office that morning and I was not asked to leave after putting my list of names on the deputy chief constable's desk. In any case I did not like losing sight of the list because it was the only one in existence and I was responsible for its safety. I remained standing behind the deputy chief constable who was sitting at his desk, while the chief superintendent was a few feet away to one side and probably could not see the actual names on the list.

One or two names were talked about for a minute or two without any sign of a decision being made. This was a bit puzzling because one man stood out head and shoulders above the rest – all were known to me personally – and yet he was not even getting a mention. He was a very experienced sergeant who had an excellent assessment report from his divisional chief superintendent and had been graded A+ by the promotion board. Not only that but he was then stationed within a few miles of the place where the inspector vacancy had arisen, and promoting him would not have involved any expense in moving him. He seemed the ideal man for the job but was not getting a look in.

It was really none of my business but eventually I could keep quiet no longer. I asked the deputy chief constable if I could make a suggestion. He agreed, and without saying any more I used my pen to draw an imaginary line under the name that for me stood out from the rest. The deputy chief constable snapped, 'Dead wrong 'un', and went back to his musings about one or two of the others on the list. I did not take much more notice.

The trouble was that anyone with a little knowledge of this particular sergeant would have known he was not a 'Dead wrong 'un' or anything like it, and it was ridiculous that one man's prejudice should be overriding everyone else's clear and stated views to deprive the service of the full potential of the man. This was to say nothing of the feelings of the individual concerned, who as I knew myself from a recent conversation with him was very frustrated and depressed about his apparent lack of any future in the job.

Another complicating factor in this case was that the divisional chief superintendent who had given the sergeant the glowing assessment was a rather too intelligent man for some influential members of the force hierarchy to feel entirely comfortable with. It was around this time that one of them tried to persuade me, unsuccessfully, that this chief super was a 'bloody old woman.' Anyway, the good news was that the sergeant did get promoted not long after the brief 'discussion' in the deputy chief constable's office.

Of course, where prejudice was concerned, it could work the other way as well. The same individualistic constable who some time earlier had been written off by a promotion board as 'an extraordinary fellow' eventually came into favour in the appropriate quarters and was now a sergeant appearing before a promotion board presided over by an assistant chief constable who was certainly not noted for his individuality. The sergeant did not endear himself to the board and in fact ended the interview with a remark that one member at least considered offensive. In subsequent discussion a suggestion that the sergeant be given a low grading was immediately over-ruled by the presiding assistant chief constable with the disclosure that, 'We can't – the deputy chief constable's going to promote him next week!'

The basic qualification for promotion to the rank of sergeant or inspector was that one should have passed the appropriate written examination and satisfied a promotion board. This still produced too many candidates for the available posts so naturally there had to be selection as well. Inevitably, it was not just a question of being good at one's job at the time but rather of getting oneself in the right place to find favour with someone you could identify as being influential in the right quarters. The best plan was to be 'well in with' your head of division or department, in the expectation that he would not only do you a good promotion board assessment report but might also put a word in for you at the selection process above the level of the promotion board. Ideally, of course, your 'middle man' should himself be popular in the upper echelons, although this was not always crucial because a loose quota system operated whereby the various divisions and departments got a roughly equal number of promotions in the long run.

Naturally, the ambitious promotion candidate could markedly improve his prospects by identifying the chief's (and also preferably the deputy chief's) off-duty interests and cultivating similar ones himself. If the chief was a church-goer then be in the right denomination and get yourself seen regularly among the congregation. Methodism, for example, was in favour at one time. A set of golf clubs would usually be a sound investment. Freemasonry was certainly worth considering but was not always of crucial importance: membership indeed was abandoned in one or two cases where that was deemed prudent in light of the chief constable's views on the brotherhood at the time.

Where one chief in particular was concerned, it was certainly best if he fancied your wife – although I hasten to say there was no need for any special contribution on her part beyond the ordinary niceties of social intercourse. Having the right make of car was important – Volvo was usually a safe bet – although it was naturally as well to be careful to go for a rather more modest model than the top man's choice. In general, conformity was the rule and any sign of individuality could be dangerous in the extreme.

Anyone with ambitions had to see the value of being stationed at force headquarters. While there was a general tendency among police staff in the out-stations to wonder about the relevance of force HQ, anyone out there who really wanted to make his mark was best advised to disabuse himself of such doubts and be seen at HQ at every possible opportunity. Even if he could not get himself appointed to something like a force working party that met regularly at HQ, then at least he could be seen at sporting and social functions there.

Conversely, any headquarters officer misguided enough to feel he could do with some police experience in the outside world had to be exceedingly wary of expressing such sentiments lest his fundamental loyalty to the job be cast in doubt. The point was of course that force HQ was the fount of all knowledge and the hub of the universe: it was there to be served by the rest of the force and not the other way round. Divisional staff involved in day-to-day policing with all its messiness and inconvenience were 'the hewers of wood and the drawers of water', while headquarters officers should see they were operating on an altogether higher plane.

Any officer at force HQ of the rank of inspector or above was entitled to join the Mess – or, rather, was obliged to join because anyone with the temerity to decline the opportunity for membership would really have been jeopardising his prospects. The Mess held occasional social functions at which it was advisable to be seen with one's wife, whether one wanted to be there or not. Having attended several of these gatherings over the years, I never thought they were a great success. There was never an easy relationship in the Mess between the various ranks – the hierarchy bearing a heavy responsibility for this – and at one stage at least there was general anxiety about assuming responsibility for organising Mess functions for fear of attracting blame for anything going wrong. One officer's sudden removal from headquarters to a far-off divisional station was attributed to his part in putting on a cracked record as musical accompaniment.

HQ Mess was open daily at appropriate times for coffee and tea. These occasions were usually attended by at least one member of the rank of assistant chief constable or above, so it was advisable for the ambitious young HQ officer to make every effort to get himself there. The generally convivial atmosphere provided a little light relief from routine, and early attendance would usually secure a seat near the bench that was traditionally reserved for the hierarchy. This of course meant that you were well placed to be seen to agree readily with any pronouncements emanating from that quarter and laugh heartily at any witticisms from the same source.

Good-natured banter would flourish when a more cautious tone was not being adopted out of deference to the presence of a high-ranking officer. One morning, for example, a middle-ranking officer, who had reputedly achieved his promotion successes through adoption of a selection of the ploys I have just touched upon above, rose from his seat with some apparent difficulty and remarked that his knees were giving him trouble. This attracted an observation to the effect that it was not surprising having regard to the amount of time he had spent on them… Still, all due credit to him – he had used 'the system' to his advantage and it was to be hoped he was happy with the outcome.

However, in making these comments (tongue-in-cheek, but only slightly) about the promotion system, I have got rather ahead of myself, so to speak. I took the written examination for promotion to inspector and managed to pass it. Actually, without being able to recall the full details, I think I must have been lucky enough to do fairly well in this exam because the chief constable himself was moved to congratulate me on the result, and I could not imagine him doing that very often.

The next step was to get myself on a promotion board. No problem there because I was responsible for organising these things. As staff officer in all but name, I was obviously in a privileged position (which I tried never to abuse, I hasten to add) and in the circumstances I was not likely to get an adverse assessment report. Equally importantly, it was my job initially to choose the two senior officers who made up the panel of each promotion board under the chairmanship of the assistant chief constable.

Anyway, early in 1974 I was surprised to be promoted inspector only two years after my previous promotion – although inspector was probably the appropriate rank for anyone acting as staff officer. By all accounts the chief constable usually addressed those appearing before him for promotion to inspector with his standard homily on the subject of dignity and standards required, such as the importance of not being seen on the street eating fish and chips from a newspaper, but he said in my case he was not going to bother with that. Perhaps he had seen me with the right newspaper. He did say, however, that it had taken him rather longer to reach the rank that he was now bestowing on me but, by Jove, I need not think I was better than he was. The thought never crossed my mind.

I was certainly not complacent, and indeed I have to reveal that I was secretly disappointed about a failure in one aspect of the brief the chief constable had given me on appointment to the staff officer function two years earlier. That is, the chief's instruction to me to look after the recently appointed assistant chief constable and my subsequent adjuration to the new man about the dangers of upsetting the chief. There was a honeymoon period between the two of them but it did not last. It all ended with the Great Furniture Incident.

'Special K', as the assistant chief constable was sometimes affectionately known (his surname beginning with K and his manner being highly polished), was not happy with his dull office furniture, so he went ahead and got it changed for something a lot brighter – mainly white in fact. The result was quite stunning in the sombre surroundings of the top landing of police headquarters and was proudly displayed by the assistant chief constable to all and sundry. Unfortunately, however, he had not taken the precaution of consulting the chief about this major change in force policy. Shortly afterwards, while the assistant chief constable was away on official business in London, the chief found out about the exotic new furniture in the office next to his. No doubt he had been tipped off.

Seeing all this as a serious challenge to his authority, the chief ordered the new office furniture to be removed and everything to be put back as it had been before. On the assistant chief constable's return a couple of days later, he was clearly shocked to find what had happened and was really never quite the same again. It was just a matter of time before he would leave Cumbria for a staff appointment at the Police College and then become Commissioner of Police in Fiji, no less.

As assistant chief constable, 'Special K' had been his own man and something of an individualist. That of course was not really what was required at that time. His replacement was a different proposition altogether. John Leslie, as he was popularly known, was a home-grown Cumbrian and as good a 'yes' man as you are ever likely to meet. Some ten years earlier, as a detective inspector, he had been involved in a murder investigation which led to the last sentence of capital punishment to be imposed in Britain, although generally his 30-odd years' police service did not appear to have been marked with any great distinction apart from a well-honed adroitness at 'watching his back' without ever sticking his neck out. It was to his credit also that he had cultivated the right social connections and enjoyed his golf – a sport in which of course he took care never to be so good as to beat anybody that mattered.

This being the mid 1970s, it was fashionable to talk about management styles – autocratic, laissez-faire and so on. Although I suppose I had the normal interest in such matters, I was never able to put John Leslie's management style into any of the standard categories that I knew of. His approach to decision-making was essentially one of 'Well, what do you think?' Whatever your response to that oft-repeated question, you always had the assurance of knowing not only that your suggestion would be received with interest and courtesy but also that it would be double (and probably treble) checked with anyone else who came to mind – or happened to come into the assistant chief constable's office after you had left. The end product of this highly developed consultation process would usually be the drafting in manuscript of a carefully worded but brief assistant chief constable's memo and its attachment to the relevant file with a paperclip (for easy removal in case of emergency). Mind you, John Leslie did have a beautiful signature. You had to give him that.

Apart from his studiousness in avoiding decisions, John Leslie never 'rocked the boat', was never there when trouble arose and always denied all knowledge if trouble seemed to be looming. A colleague of mine at this time happened to be the force recruiting officer and as such was closely involved with John Leslie in the assistant chief constable's capacity as senior officer responsible for appointment of new police recruits. After going through all the due processes, a young woman had been appointed to the force and was about to begin her initial training when medical opinion was received to the effect that she was pregnant. This appalling news about a new recruit was greeted by John Leslie with his instinctive reaction to trouble, based on years of experience: 'Well, I'm not responsible for this!' Fortunately, it turned out to be a false alarm, so the question of responsibility, in whatever sense, did not arise in this case.

John Leslie's prowess at showing deference to the chief was impressive. No matter that the chief was inclined to poke fun at our hero – he had still made the rank of assistant chief constable. The two of them were on the golf course one fine day and John Leslie was making a hash of his swing, possibly because he was being watched by the chief. The chief observed the inept performance resignedly for a while and then said, 'Why not tell us a story, Smithers? You're better at that.'

Just as John Leslie was deferential to the point of self-effacement, he was uncomprehending of anyone less polished in that respect. The assistant chief constable's office was next to the chief's, and discussions there were usually conducted quietly with the door closed, in case the great man next door should hear anything untoward. It was approaching lunch-time one day and I happened to be with the assistant chief constable in his office when the door opened. We had not heard anyone coming but it was the chief himself. The assistant chief constable was a good 20 years my senior but he was out of his chair and rigidly to attention quicker than I was.

The chief came in. Was it to be some issue of high force policy that he would raise with the assistant chief constable? No, it was me he addressed with his best West Country burr, albeit solemnly: 'Sharpe', he said, 'tell me. Whoy is it? Whoy is it' (he tended to repeat himself for emphasis when the gravity of the occasion demanded) 'that your woife is so much better looking than you are?'

Unabashed, I looked the chief in the eye and replied with equal solemnity, 'Well, sir, I do have other less obvious talents.' The chief permitted himself a trace of a smile and sauntered off down the stairs. John Leslie was aghast at my temerity.

Talking about the inimitable John Leslie and the subject of deference brings to mind the Halford case that caught the attention of the media some time later. Some people may remember Miss Alison Halford, ex-Metropolitan Police and an out-of-the-ordinary assistant chief constable of Merseyside, who brought an action against her own chief constable and Police Authority on grounds of sex discrimination arising out of her failure to be promoted to the rank of deputy chief constable. Her grievance apparently was based on her shock at finding the promotion she wanted had gone to a fellow assistant chief constable (male) whom she regarded as far less qualified than herself. A significant stage of the tribunal hearing was reported in the *Daily Express*.

Assuming Miss Halford's comments about Mr David Howe were reported accurately, I cannot help feeling they were a bit naive. I have regard particularly to the phrases 'he came in on my coat tails'; 'of those interviewed for the post, he was the least competent'; 'his background was in Cumbria – all tourists and sheep farming'; 'he wasn't a leader'; and 'he was in great fear of the chief constable.' Surely, Miss Halford, with the greatest respect, if these things were true – particularly the last of them, in my view – then Mr Howe did not get his promotion to deputy chief constable in Merseyside in spite of them, as you suggest, but precisely because of them. Logic would perhaps dictate that he should have been congratulated on the success of his tactics rather than criticised for them.

I should explain that I followed the press reports of the sensational Halford case of the early 1990s with more than a passing interest because the late Mr David Howe joined the police service in Cumbria the same day as I did and indeed was one of the five other young men who stood with me in the stores at Police HQ at Penrith to be kitted out that fateful day in January 1963. Knowing him as I did, I could well understand the critical observations about him that were attributed to Miss Halford, but he achieved at least some of his perhaps surprising advancements in the police service by much the same middle of the road tactics as were adopted by our worthy assistant chief constable, John Leslie, in earlier years. The advantages David Howe may have had over Miss Halford were that he was an ex-police cadet (and therefore nicely steeped in the conformity culture from an impressionable age), he had long been immersed in the rituals of the estimable Brotherhood and, crucially, his earlier promotions among Cumbria's sheep and tourists had been achieved under a supreme autocrat of the same ilk as the then chief constable of Merseyside.

Once again, however, I am getting a bit ahead of myself, so to speak. It was still the mid-1970s and life with the promotion board material, complaint files and so on had to go on. People generally at this time were becoming more inclined to question authority in all its forms, and this trend was being reflected in increasing numbers of complaints against police. Most forces by then had a headquarters department to deal specifically with such matters, thereby keeping the whole issue centralised under the deputy chief constable and relieving senior divisional officers of the problem. The departmental title of complaints and discipline was one I never liked because I thought it sounded unnecessarily ominous, but I could not think of an adequate alternative.

Anyway, trailing perhaps a little way behind most other police forces (and is that necessarily a bad thing?), Cumbria got its own Complaints and Discipline Department. This was achieved gradually over a period of months with the transfer in of a chief inspector first, then a superintendent and me. Actually, for me it did not involve much of a change, because initially at least I still carried on with most of my staff officer functions, including administration of complaints and discipline matters, although it did enable me to get out 'in the field' rather more than I had been used to recently, and that suited me fine. Perhaps we had not quite got our terms of reference clear because a rather embarrassing problem

Painting of Bramshill Police College in Hampshire.

soon arose.

For three years or so I had worked directly for the deputy chief constable and, to a rather lesser extent, the assistant chief, from an office on the top landing near to theirs. With establishment of the complaints and discipline department, I found myself transferred to fresh quarters on the ground floor at the far end of the force headquarters building, where I was joined by two new colleagues, the chief inspector and the superintendent.

I had been used to working very much on my own initiative. In particular, all papers relating to complaints and discipline matters were passed by the force administration department straight to me. Knowing that the deputy chief constable wanted answers, not questions (and respecting that point of view), my normal practice was just to anticipate his decision in each case and then go ahead and prepare the necessary paperwork for his signature. Experience had shown the system to work perfectly well in nine cases out of ten, and if there was a disagreement then naturally alterations were made to suit what the deputy chief wanted.

The new superintendent was not only an ex-cadet – here I go again, showing my prejudice against these people – but he came from a divisional station where personal initiative was discouraged and rank was all-important. Quite understandably in the absence of any guidance from above, he saw me not so much as staff officer, which I had never been officially designated anyway, but simply as a member of his department.

The inevitable outcome was that all material relating to complaints and discipline now went to him in the first instance instead of to me, and he assumed responsibility for consulting the deputy chief in such matters. With his background it was perfectly natural for him to gather together all the relevant papers on a daily basis and report first thing to the deputy chief's office for instruction as to how to proceed in this often delicate area. This is how the police force normally works, although I suppose he could have asked me how the system had been running previously; anyway, he didn't ask. Where he came from, superintendents would hardly ask inspectors what to do.

For a short while the new superintendent 'went upstairs' at 9am daily with his pile of papers to consult the oracle, reappearing half an hour or so later to pass on the received wisdom (or such of it as he saw fit to divulge) to his minions who were eagerly awaiting his return back in the office in the nether regions of the force headquarters complex. As a long-term divisional officer, he must have been quite pleased to find himself having the opportunity for a daily tete-a-tete with the all-powerful deputy chief.

One morning shortly after 9am I was at my desk. The office door was open and I could see my new-found friend the superintendent coming along the corridor, carrying an impressive bundle of papers and wearing an even more lugubrious expression than usual. He dumped his burden on my desk and said, 'He's bloody chased me. You'd better get yourself upstairs with this lot. He must be in love with you.' He sat down, dejected. Maybe I felt a bit sorry for him, maybe not. With his impatient disposition and incisively critical way with words that had probably been honed during his time in the Military Police, the deputy chief was not an easy man to deal with.

I picked up the files and set off on the long trek up to the deputy chief's office via all the flights of stairs and self-closing firedoors. Reaching the deputy's office a few minutes later, I was greeted with a look as black as thunder.

Deputy chief constable: 'Where the hell have you been? I've hardly seen you for weeks.'

Me: 'Sorry, sir. I have a superintendent over me now, and I thought. . .'

Deputy chief constable: 'Never mind about that. You always used to be in my office two or three times a day at least. Nothing has changed as far as I'm concerned. I want to see you in here.'

Well, I suppose things were now a bit clearer. I went back to my corner to get on with the job of anticipating the deputy's decisions on the day's paperwork and having the answers ready for his signature, as I had been used to doing for the past three years. The deputy chief constable obviously wanted things to stay that way; I didn't blame him for that and the method suited me fine. The morning's events did leave a bit of an 'atmosphere' in our little world for a day or two, but we got over it. And something else soon turned up to take me away from things for a while – the Inspectors' Course at the Police College.

Not everybody knows this (as Michael Caine might have said), but deep in the sylvan Hampshire countryside stood an imposing red-brick Jacobean mansion that looked out over tranquil parkland of grazing deer and honking geese. This was Bramshill Police College where the chosen few of the police service were supposed to escape the hurly-burly of day-to-day policing for a time and contemplate the broader issues of their calling.

After a 300-mile drive down from Cumbria I arrived at the college in March 1976. I was one of over a hundred hopefuls from all parts of the country who were beginning the same three-month course. Day-to-day activities consisted of lectures, syndicate discussions, presentations, simulated exercises and so on; and you were always conscious of being watched in 'class' and marked accordingly to staff assessment of your contribution. Amassing your tally of 'grovel points' was the thing, in the knowledge that a report was going back to your chief constable at the end of the course.

Right at the start we were put under a bit of pressure by having several topics thrown at us for written presentation, with completion deadlines set at intervals throughout the course, and one or two subjects also for oral delivery. My topics included 'Nature and role of Police in a liberal democratic society' and 'Crowd Behaviour', along with more arcane subjects like 'Britain's interest in a Rhodesian settlement' and 'Comprehensive education will not improve academic standards'. A perhaps particularly surprising one in the context of a police course was that I was required to do an essay on the nineteenth century thinker John Stuart Mill's views about the importance of promoting diversity and individuality. The great man was evidently concerned about society's pressures to conform and felt that real progress in human affairs was only possible through free expression of individuality. With ideas like that, Mr Mill would never have got anywhere in the police force!

It was an interesting three months with an ambitious programme, although the place did leave me with mixed feelings about its chances of long-term success. Despite what must have been a sizeable budget, the accommodation was barely adequate and overcrowding was always apparent. The college's pretensions to academic status had to be viewed against the day-to-day practicalities of policing, and policemen generally were not over-keen to go there either as students or staff. Then again, in a system of policing giving so much autonomy to each chief constable and police authority, attendance at the college was no guarantee of success in the promotion stakes any more than failure to get there was a bar to advancement.

A few days after I got back to Cumbria from the college the chief constable sent for me. He had my report in front of him and was good enough to congratulate me on it. Then suddenly he said, 'Tell me, Sharpe, what is wrong with the Police College?' I passed some comment about the place lacking a sense of inspiration and purpose, which seemed to find favour, but hastened to add that I was nevertheless grateful for the opportunity to go there.

Back on familiar territory, I reflected on the fact that I had been working in the cloistered environs of force headquarters for some years, and it was perhaps time for a change. Putting that idea into effect, however, was a different matter entirely. Clearly, I was in close touch with the people who mattered most in the organisation and was 'in a good seam', as they used to say. Perhaps I should have been content to press on regardless, but I was becoming disenchanted with a role somewhere between ghost writer and *eminence grise*.

Looking back on it, I suppose I joined the job to be a policeman and still had not quite got that naive notion out of my head. The danger of such ideas, of course, was that in an individual of any apparent academic ability they were liable to be interpreted as lack of ambition or even as some sort of inverted snobbery. Even more serious was the question of loyalty: anyone with a grace and favour appointment like mine would surely imply disloyalty to his betters if he tried to raise the possibility of going somewhere else.

There was a uniformed patrol inspector at the local town police station who was past the first flush of youth, and I knew from a surreptitious look at his personal record that he would be obliged to retire on his 60th birthday some six months hence. While I hankered after his job, in the circumstances I lacked the resolve to ask for it. However, one day soon afterwards I was in the deputy chief constable's office.

The immediate business had been dealt with and I was about to leave when the deputy chief coughed, looked rather uncomfortable and said, 'Do you know you're moving?' I said I didn't and he went on to say, nodding towards the chief constable's office over the corridor: 'He's sending you to Penrith, to Inspector Little's job when he retires.' I was surprised, but this of course was the very job I had been thinking about these past few months but had never found the courage to ask for. I could not look elated at the prospect, for the reasons outlined above – and I certainly did not want to offend the deputy chief constable – so I decided to appear impassive. The deputy chief constable looked down and went on, 'You don't have to go if you don't want to.' Searching for the right response, I replied, 'That's all right, sir. If I'm required to go, I'll just get on with it.'

The couple of weeks or so left to me at force HQ gave

me time to reflect. It was fourteen years since I joined the police and the job had altered somewhat. In our confrontation with the motorist we had acquired traffic wardens, double yellow lines all over the place, radar speedmeters and a lot more traffic patrol vehicles.

In towns you didn't see anything like as many policemen about as you used to but they did have panda cars and personal radios to get them to trouble quicker (and get them back-up if they got there too soon), along with big blue vans to carry the prisoners in and the beginnings of computer systems to record it all on. Specialised departments were burgeoning and the civilian staff were growing apace. All this drive for organisational efficiency might have been a bit expensive but it must be a good thing, surely?

The trouble was, the police service didn't seem to be accepted by press and public as readily as it had been a few years earlier, and police evidence was becoming more likely to be successfully challenged in court. It just didn't seem to be a 'bobby's job' any more, and it was even becoming fashionable to talk about stress in the police service. The only yardstick they seemed able to find for measuring police efficiency was the crime rate (rising) and detection rate (falling).

Still, if the general situation was getting worse, at least it fuelled well-meaning demands for more tools to do the job and more police pay, so why worry? On the personal front, the job had been good to me. With only one enforced move of residence I had been promoted twice, and due recognition had usually been given to such talents and experience as I thought I had. In return I had tried to do a loyal and conscientious job and at least I felt I had put a lot of effort into it. Once or twice perhaps I had erred on the individualistic side but it did not seem to have done me any harm.

5
THE SUB-DIVISION

In mid-February 1977 I cleared out the accumulated paraphernalia from my desk at force headquarters and transferred it to my new quarters a mile or so away in the town police station. A small market town with a population of around 12,000, Penrith did rate the status of a sub-divisional headquarters because it was at the centre of a large rural area roughly corresponding with the ethereal-sounding Eden District. While it did have a lot of 'sheep and tourists', it also had about 20 miles of the M6 motorway running through the middle, along with around 40 miles of the A66 trunk road and also the main London-Glasgow railway line, so it was not completely off the beaten track. Home Secretary Willie Whitelaw was the local MP and lived just outside the town, so we could regard ourselves as a safe Tory seat.

The superintendent in charge of the sub-division was an ex-Army man with a keen interest in guns. He was in fact the senior force firearms instructor and the man who was always consulted and called in to take charge of firearms incidents throughout the force area. (These things did happen occasionally, although nothing in my experience on the scale of the 1965 Oxenholme incident). Ours being very much a rural area, a lot of farmers and other people had firearms and shotguns so there was considerable involvement for the police in supervision of such matters for licensing purposes and issue of certificates. Far be it from me to suggest our superintendent was dogmatic but he did regard himself as the authority on firearms, bar none.

It is fair to say that the sub-divisional superintendent did not give me a whole-hearted welcome to his little domain. It may be that he had had someone else in mind for the vacancy that had arisen on his staff, but his coolness towards me was more likely due to the fact that I had come from force HQ. Worse, he would have known that my move to his station had been instigated by the chief constable himself, and it was soon clear to me that he did not like the chief at all – indeed that he lived in fear of the man. It was no wonder that my arrival was something less than good news for him. Perhaps he even saw me as an HQ spy with a direct line to the top.

It was to the superintendent's credit, though, that he usually let me get on with the job without undue interference. On the question of his pet subject, I remember once it transpired that a firearm belonging to no less a figure than Willie Whitelaw had gone missing when a constable went to check on it at certificate renewal time. Mr Whitelaw could not account for it and the possibility of proceedings against him was starting to arise. This was causing a bit of nervousness in some quarters and there were people who were content to leave the young constable who had raised the problem to struggle on with it on his own. The superintendent, however, showed his mettle by announcing, 'Yes, well, he'll be treated no differently from any other Home Secretary!' Fortunately the missing weapon did turn up eventually so nobody's resolve had to be put to the test.

The town uniformed patrol staff consisted of one other inspector in addition to me, a few sergeants and about 20 constables, and there were two traffic wardens. I had been away from 'ordinary outside police duty' for some time, so I was prepared to keep as low a profile as possible at first. Trying to crack eggs with a big stick was never my style anyway, and this new situation was certainly not the occasion for such antics. I had only been in post for about two hours and was hoping nothing dramatic would happen just yet when a very talkative woman was shown into my office – to make a complaint against police. What a relief! I say that because with my experience in that particular field over the past few years that was one area in which I felt more than comfortable. Anyway, I managed to smooth things over and the lady eventually left the station without anything going on paper.

Any complacency I might have felt about this early success 'in the field' was soon shattered when I found myself literally in a field with a case of foot-and-mouth disease. 'Diseases of Animals' was a recurring problem in a rural area, and the police at that time had appreciable involvement. My experience in such matters lay somewhere between nil and very rusty, but a sergeant friend of mine sorted it all out on this occasion while I purported to supervise him.

I mentioned before that there were about 20 constables in the town – on shifts, of course, so there were never more than four or five available at any one time. The main problem, though, was that they were nearly all probationers – that is, new starters in their first two years' service. At one particularly low point in fact there was only one uniformed constable available for outside duty who was not a probationer! While the town was not exactly the Wild West, having so many learners to deal with things inevitably meant that even minor incidents could often be hard work for supervisory staff. Policing at first can often feel like a matter of trial and error with more error than anything else.

Then again, about a third of the constables were young ladies and, with the greatest respect to them, they could bring their own set of problems. One young woman had been with us a week or two when her shift sergeant came into my office and took care to shut the door firmly behind him. 'Got a real problem here' was the sergeant's opener.

He went on to say that the young woman, who was on duty in uniform, had simply vanished in broad daylight. He had been trying for over two hours to find her by calling her on the personal radio system and scouring the streets on foot. No trace. He was very worried about her. So was I now. This was a new one on me. The Police College had had some pretty way-out stuff on the agenda but I could not think of anything there to help me with this one. (Well, what would you do if somebody went missing and you were seriously worried about them – tell the police? This was one of those times when you think to yourself, 'My God, I am the police.')

As we pondered the problem, the 'phone rang. It was the proprietor of a town cafe who was well known to us as the supplier of prisoners' meals. He sounded rather worried and puzzled. He told me that a cubicle in the ladies' toilets at his premises had been locked from the inside for some time. There was someone in there and they were getting concerned to the extent that his staff had tried to attract the attention of this person but got no response. Further than that, a gap under the door revealed what looked like a policewoman's bag and personal radio…

The sergeant went round to the cafe and confirmed that it was indeed our missing policewoman but he could not get her to come out. The only other female on duty at the station at the time was a young cadet. She was quite a sensible girl for her tender years, so I sent her to the scene to see what she could do. She was eventually successful in getting the door open, and about half an hour later she arrived back at the station with the young policewoman and the sergeant.

The young woman had reasonable reports from the police training centre, but she had found it quite a shock to go out in public in uniform. Eventually she had lost her nerve and hid herself in the cafe toilet. To make matters worse, she had been drinking from a bottle of gin and was rather the worse for wear. Perhaps further complicating matters, while she was trying to compose herself, a rather shady-looking character with a large car arrived at the police station and asked for the address of her lodgings. It seemed he was a Lancashire man she had been seeing while she was at the initial police training centre and he had taken it upon himself to come to Penrith and look her up. I saw him myself and he left shortly afterwards without getting the information he wanted.

By now it was nearing the young woman's shift finishing time for that day, so I arranged for someone to take her home. Clearly things were not going to work out for her in the police force, so before she left the station I suggested pointedly to her that she should give serious consideration to her position and come in the following morning when she had made up her mind what she wanted to do. In the meantime there would be nothing going on paper about what had happened that day. She came in next day and put in her resignation, which was no doubt best for all concerned.

The Employment Protection laws did not apply to the police force. Police regulations provided that a probationer police officer's services could be dispensed with at any time if he or she did not seem likely to make the grade. While there was always a danger of this provision being used as a threat to induce a probationer to resign against his/her will, in my experience it seemed a necessary safeguard for the police and was not invoked too often. After the initial two-year probationary period was up it was not too easy to get rid of a police officer who was not pulling his weight.

Police officers in general must have been just about the easiest people to manage because nobody joined to be a subversive but among all the conformity the job did not find it easy to accommodate and motivate the occasional individual who did not quite fit in. It seemed easier to write him off as a trouble-maker without bothering to reflect on where the problem might lie. Extending the argument a little bit, I am reminded of the pragmatic observation of a hoary old superintendent about a recently-retired sergeant who, as a man of some ability and intelligence, might have been expected to have gone a bit higher in the job than he did: 'He didn't kowtow so he didn't get on.' I surmised that the sergeant had probably not said 'Sir' often enough to the hoary old superintendent who was telling me the tale.

However, to get back from the intricacies of police management in general to the particular problems presented by the young ladies. One morning a female probationer who should have started in on the early turn at 6am rang in to say she was reporting sick with a heavy cold. The call was duly recorded and placed on the general station message file. The next call about her condition was the following day from a hospital maternity unit, where she had given birth.

Personally, I had not seen the poor girl for a few weeks because of the way her shifts had been running in relation to mine, but none of us had had any idea of the problem she had, not even another policewoman who was lodging with her. She was a big girl and I suppose we all thought that was all there was to it; but she had been on ordinary outside duty right up to the day she got her 'heavy cold', and the implications were alarming. Nevertheless, a particularly thick-skinned senior officer made light of the situation by taking the opportunity over the next day or two of asking other young policewomen whether they had a cough.

I would hate it to be thought from these remarks that I am some sort of misogynist. Nothing could be further from the truth. It is just that I was never happy about bringing so many young women into the police service at the same time. Going back to my early days in the job at my first station, there was only one policewoman there at that time. Her conditions of service were rather different from the men's, and her primary concerns were the problems of women and children. In the meantime the Sex Discrimination laws had obliged the police to abolish their system of separate establishments for women and introduce total integration.

The problems really began at the recruit selection stage because quite a lot of young women naturally saw the police job as an attractive proposition, and their paper qualifications were likely to look at least as good as those of the male applicants. At the interview stage it was largely a matter of 'presence', and my experience of sitting on recruiting panels was that the women applicants often came over better than their male counterparts. (Mind you, every such panel I ever sat on was composed entirely of men, so we did have the obvious problem of trying to be dispassionate in these matters).

One source of recruitment that always did leave me unimpressed was the cadet system, as will have become clear from comments I have passed on it before. Maybe it was a rather unusual problem but during my time in the sub-division we had the case of the transvestite cadet.

We had a young man aged about seventeen who had been with us a matter of weeks as the station police cadet. He was a courteous and tidy lad but perhaps rather quiet. One dark night two policemen travelling in a vehicle on a country road just outside the town noticed what appeared to be a tall young woman walking on her own. Being anxious for her safety, they stopped to see if there was a problem; but then they started to get concerned about this individual's gender, despite the full female attire including the dress and high-heels.

On the way to the town station in the police car the young person asked the two policemen, 'Do you not recognise me?'

They didn't and were enlightened with the information, 'Well, I'm the station cadet!' For some reason best known to himself, the lad had got himself into a full outfit of his mother's and had set off on a nocturnal walk. Maybe he had not really wanted to join the police and this was some form of protest. Anyway, we had no use for a cadet in drag so the unfortunate lad's services were immediately terminated. I understand he joined the Navy soon afterwards.

Having responsibility for so many learners at a station only a mile or so from police headquarters could itself bring problems. One such diplomatic incident sticks in my mind (and rather stuck in my throat at the time) as the affair of the strawberries.

A coachload of beer-swilling football supporters had been passing through the town when they found the collective need to pass something else. The driver stopped to let them out, and an outraged local resident rang the police to complain about the resulting urinary defilement of his front garden. A very young policeman was despatched to the scene. Whether the direct evidence of the felony had ceased to exist by the time he got there or whether, being completely outnumbered, he had decided to remove his helmet and mingle with the crowd, I know not. However, our young hero's efforts to deal with the situation had certainly not impressed the complainant, who voiced his displeasure to the deputy chief constable, who happened to be a member of the same Rotary club as himself.

While I had not actually been on duty at the time of the incident, I soon found myself at force HQ in the deputy chief constable's office being harangued on the correct method of handling a piddling bunch of football supporters and on my own apparent failure to treat the whole thing as seriously as it clearly deserved to be. Oh dear, oh dear, it's tough at the top.

More seriously, though, if we were going to review what

happened here, then we really should have been asking not so much what this very young policeman did or did not do but rather why it was necessary to send someone so utterly inexperienced on his own. No doubt the answer to that would have been that there was simply no one else to send. So often in policing it was not a question of what you did or did not do that counted but rather of looking as if you knew what you were doing, and that only came with experience. But the fundamental problem here, of course, was why we had to be trying to police the town with so many probationers. For me to have raised that obvious point about force organisation and priorities would not just have been a matter of rocking the boat; it would have been capsizing it with me underneath.

However, back to everyday matters. One constantly recurring commitment that always had to take precedence even over staff problems was court work. This being the 1970s, it was before the introduction of the Crown Prosecution Service, and the police themselves were responsible for handling virtually all their own cases in the magistrates' courts. At this time in the sub-division there were no less than five separate magistrates' courts scattered about the area. As prosecuting officer, the town inspector had to attend two of them on a regular weekly basis, and he could find himself in any of the other three as well, sometimes at very short notice if the local man was not available for any reason. Familiarising oneself beforehand with the often quite bulky court file and then presenting all the cases at the subsequent proceedings probably took up nearly half the inspector's time on average. I remember in one exceptional run my record was six courts in six days including a special hearing on a Saturday morning.

Prosecuting in court could be quite demanding at times, and of course there was no training for it. You just had to pick up the court file and plunge in at the deep end, to learn by experience as best you could.

The reason for the five different magistrates' courts in a thinly-populated and mainly rural area was all to do with a system of local justice that went back a long way. For centuries this form of summary jurisdiction had been known as the petty sessions (literally 'small sittings', I suppose from the Norman-French) and you sometimes could not help thinking they were aptly-named in view of the seriousness or otherwise of some of the cases they dealt with.

A few years after my time all of these small local courts were closed down. Although of course the law they were administering was the same, their methods could vary considerably. Each court was run by its own magistrates' clerk, a local solicitor whose job it was to advise the lay magistrates on the relevant law, and the subtle differences between the various courts were largely attributable to the approach adopted by the clerk in each case.

For me, the most far-flung outpost of the magistracy was based about 25 miles away in delightfully Dickensian quarters at the rear of a small police station. It only sat about once a month because that was how long it took in the area to drum up enough business to justify a sitting. The rather elderly clerk was one of the most courteous gentlemen I have ever met, always infinitely solicitous for the interests of all concerned but especially for the defendant in each case. More than once I saw him persuade a defendant who had pleaded guilty to change his plea to not guilty and come back to a later hearing when he had taken legal advice.

The pace of proceedings in this gentleman's court was always exceedingly leisurely. Indeed, he took the view that court business must always last until lunchtime at least since otherwise it would not have been worthwhile troubling the Bench to attend. It was all very nice but you could get a bit fidgety if you had things on your mind 'back home' to deal with.

The required pace was precisely the opposite at the main magistrates' court in the area. The clerk here was a very clever man who did not suffer fools gladly, and his purpose was always to get the court business over with as fast as possible so that he could get back to his office in private practice (which was no doubt more lucrative than sitting in court). The clerk he usually brought with him to look after the papers and collect the fines and so on (yes, there was a magistrates' clerk's clerk) was a middle-aged man of an anxious disposition who appeared to be on a substantial dose of medication for his nervous disorder and was inclined to nod off if things went quiet. I was sitting in court, facing the two of them one morning at a distance of about two feet, when poor Tommy's eyes closed and his head drooped. He was well away when our impatient clerk prodded him with his elbow and snapped his surname in his ear. Tommy woke with a start, clearly shocked, and knocked the court papers all over the floor.

But the court where anything could happen used to sit weekly in a hill village about ten miles from my base. The magistrates met halfway along the windswept main street in a converted school building with a sign outside that read simply Courthouse – a setting that would conjure up visions of the Wild West. The clerk in this case was a most charming man who usually tried not to let the court business interfere unduly with his reading of the *Daily Telegraph*.

On the face of it, this particular court only served an area full of sheep and not many tourists, but it did have a fifteen mile stretch of the M6 motorway running through it so there were usually quite a lot of driving cases. In fact, that was about 95% of the court's business. The vast majority of cases were dealt with by 'statement of facts' after a plea of guilty by post, and justice therefore was normally dispensed quite rapidly. Often there were no members of the public present, and off-hand I can't remember a press representative finding his way there either. Usually it was a question of the clerk reading out the defendant's name followed by 'speeding' or whatever, me reading the brief statement of facts, the clerk reading out the defendant's letter of mitigation (or, more likely, an extract from it that struck him as particularly funny, the quote being prefaced with a chortle and 'Cor, listen to this…') and the chairman of the Bench then announcing the penalty imposed. A couple of dozen cases could be disposed of in as many minutes by this means.

Not guilty pleas were very rare at this court – and were exceedingly unlikely to succeed since the magistrates' relations with the local police were so good that they appeared to take it for granted that the police would not have brought the charge unless the defendant was guilty.

Anyone with the temerity to plead not guilty at this Courthouse was shown into the dock. This applied whatever the nature of the alleged offence. I particularly remember a smartly dressed young man who had appeared in person to plead not guilty to speeding on the motorway. He had probably never been in a court in his life before and looked very apprehensive.

The police evidence was heard and the young man was allowed out of the dock to give his side of the story before the Bench retired to consider their decision. The defendant than resumed his seat in the dock and the clerk got on with his *Telegraph*. Those of us who were familiar with the conduct of proceedings at this court knew we would be able to relax for at least ten minutes since that was apparently how long it took the chairman to smoke a Senior Service cigarette.

All was quiet in the courtroom. Sitting twiddling my thumbs, I could see the poor defendant in the dock to my left was getting more and more anxious about the delay. Eventually he plucked up the courage to speak and, leaning over the side of the dock, he said to the clerk, 'Excuse me, sir, but what are they doing out there?'

The clerk did not look up or change his expression but simply turned over a page of his *Telegraph* and replied in a matter-of-fact tone, 'Fixing up the gibbet in the back yard for you!' Being in full uniform and not wishing to be seen as having any part in this misplaced frivolity, I cowered down in my seat. I cannot remember the result of the case but no doubt it was guilty as usual and a fine. *Fiat justitia*, as one might say.

The end of the day's business was usually heralded by the clerk gathering up his *Daily Telegraph* and court papers with the announcement, 'Right, let's get this show on the road!' He would then jump into his sporty VW Scirocco coupe for the ten-mile dash north up the A6 road to his office in Penrith while I would be expected to take up the challenge in the humble sub-divisional Mini (but of course I did have my Class 1 police driving certificate dated 1971 to even things out).

Before leaving the subject of this now defunct but particularly memorable court up in sheep country, I should say that not all the cases were motoring infringements. A somewhat troubled local youth with a history of minor indecency offences was appearing on a charge of indecent exposure. Two tough young ladies from the Glasgow area had been hitch-hiking south along the main road through the village when our friend stopped in his mini-van to pick them up. Grateful for the lift in bleak country, the pair got in and the vehicle headed off south. They had only gone a short distance when one of the young ladies noticed that their good

Samaritan had no trousers on. They yelled at him to stop the van, and as they hurriedly took their leave one of them, who had been taking note of her surroundings, told him, 'You want to get yourself a bloody sheep, mate!'

The feckless lad pleaded guilty to the offence and stood sheepishly in the dock to be fined and given a right dressing-down by the chairman of the Bench on the lines of, 'You'd better pull yourself together.' No namby-pamby suggestions like treatment for nervous disorder or counselling in this part of the world.

Anyone concerned enough about this young man's problem to wonder whether the Scottish lassie's diagnostic flair or the chairman's stern admonition were effective in preventing further untoward incidents will be disappointed to learn that they were not. Not long afterwards he exposed himself to a young off-duty nurse, who was so little moved by the performance that she asked our hero whether he could not do better than that. In fact she apparently considered the incident such a little thing that she did not report it to the police officially, although she did tell her father, a police colleague of mine, and he passed it on to me just after the event. The description given rang a bell with me and the culprit was soon apprehended.

'Flashers' are not usually dangerous but they can be quite persistent pests, and I suppose you can never be sure they will not progress to something more serious, so it is no doubt right that women offended by such antics should report the circumstances as soon as possible.

Talking about the intellectual challenge of court work puts me in mind, perhaps rather perversely, of a trip down to Preston in Lancashire for riot training, of all things. This highly physical activity among the riot shields and flying missiles was my first experience of its kind, and for me fell between two quite full days in court. The contrast could not have been more pronounced and left me thinking that perhaps rather too wide a range of skills was being expected of the police. In any case we had certainly never had a riot in Cumbria in my lifetime, let alone my time in the police there, and I don't think I was aware of an actual recent riot occurring anywhere else in the country. There had been one or two major public disturbances over the last few years, in London particularly, but nothing to my knowledge that justified the sort of protective equipment and aggressive-looking tactics we were practising with here.

Within a few years, however, we got the riots, and soon afterwards we lost the court work, with the introduction of county prosecuting solicitors' departments, which developed into the Crown Prosecution Service under the Director of Public Prosecutions.

Apart from life with the probationers and the magistrates' courts, the main recurring theme was Death: on the hills, the lakes and the roads. Any sudden death for which a doctor could not issue a certificate as to cause was a matter for the coroner for the area, and the police carried out the necessary enquiries on his behalf.

Helvellyn and Ullswater were in our area. All very scenic, obviously, and a natural attraction for people from far and wide, but they could bring sudden death to the unprepared and the unwary.

One of the saddest cases of tragedy on the lake that I remember happened on a fine spring morning just after I moved to the town station. A man and his twelve-year old daughter had set out in their small boat to row across the lake. It was a little over half a mile and the water was quite calm. They were within 50 yards of the other side when for some reason they both finished up in the water. Someone managed to get the little girl onto the shore but when I arrived on the scene at the same time as the doctor she was dead, and there was nothing the doctor could do except pronounce life extinct.

There was no sign of her father at this stage but his body was recovered from about ten feet of water the following day. Neither of them had been wearing a life jacket, and the man was wearing a heavy pair of Wellington boots that must have dragged him straight to the bottom. Exactly what happened was unclear but possibly the little girl had fallen into the water and her father jumped in to try and save her.

At just over 3,000 feet, Helvellyn is not much over an hour's walk for the reasonably fit; and on a fine day the view from the top is quite stunning, encompassing most of the main Lake District mountains and quite a few of the lakes as well. From the east, however, the approaches to the summit are quite rough with steep drops on both sides, and the place should never be taken for granted even in fine weather. If there is any snow or ice about then it can be positively treacherous, and anyone attempting the mountain in such conditions should be clear about the precautions to be taken.

One bitterly cold December day there was a light covering of snow – no more than an inch or two generally – on the hills over about the 1,000 foot contour. A party from the local Outward Bound School were on an instructional exercise near the top of Helvellyn when they saw a lone figure moving briskly in the distance, apparently running up the mountainside. They then saw the figure slip and fall several hundred feet from a ridge. There was no chance of surviving such a fall.

The Outward Bound School party recovered the body and brought it down to a shed forming part of some old mine workings on the mountainside. There was a rough road leading up to that point, and I went up there with a colleague in a police van to bring the body back to the mortuary. It was a young man, probably in his late twenties, and what struck me immediately was what he had been wearing – or, probably more to the point, not wearing. Despite the wintry conditions he had on only a tee-shirt, jeans and trainers. He had obviously been a very fit young man but he was now very dead.

The man was from Lancashire and later on we found his car parked in the village at the foot of the mountain. It seemed he was something of a fitness fanatic who liked to get in his car when the opportunity arose and come up to the Lake District to run on the hills. It was a shame he did not have a good think about what to wear, on this occasion at least.

Road accidents were the commonest cause of sudden death. 'Fatals', as such accidents were called in the police force, had been steadily declining in numbers over the years, perhaps surprisingly in view of the rapid increase in traffic volumes, but this was not much consolation to a family affected by such an event. Probably one of the main reasons for the reduction in fatal accidents has been better roads. Despite the occasional bad publicity, a motorway is by far the safest road to travel on, although of course if anything does go wrong the consequences can be that much more serious on a motorway because of the generally higher speeds involved.

A lorry had broken down on the M6 motorway near the town and was stationary on the hard shoulder when it was hit from behind by a saloon car. The middle-aged couple in the car sustained terrible head injuries and must have died instantly. The two bodies were brought to the mortuary at the back of the police station, where our lady mortuary attendant set about trying to make them look presentable. An hour or so later she told me she had finished the job and invited me to inspect her handiwork. She was quite proud of what she had done and I had to agree she had done a good job.

My next task was to arrange for the two deceased to be formally identified by next-of-kin, in this case their son. He had been told about the accident by his local police and arrived at the police station later that morning. He was a young man in his twenties and was understandably very shocked. I spent some time with him trying to prepare him for the ordeal of making the identification but the poor fellow just could not face it. In the end I had to get the necessary formality done by the family's local vicar, who had known the couple very well.

As already noted, any sudden unexplained death automatically became a matter for the coroner, and the first thing the coroner looked for was evidence of identification. While these things were not everyday occurrences, they did keep happening and a patrol inspector quite often found himself having to make the necessary arrangements. Obviously, formal identification of a body was normally done soon after the event, when the full implications of what had happened may not have fully sunk in, but generally I was deeply impressed by the courage most people showed in these distressing circumstances.

One morning I started duty at 9am to find that a motorway accident had happened during the night, in which the two occupants of a heavy lorry had died when the vehicle veered off the carriageway and came to a full-stop against a bridge abutment. Within minutes of my arrival at the station, I had a terribly distressed Scottish lady on the telephone, screaming abuse at me because the police had not been to tell her that her husband had been killed.

What had happened apparently was that a message about the accident had been sent from us to the Scottish police force concerned. This was during the night, and by the time their man got to the house to tell this unfortunate woman about the death of her husband, she had had an unofficial caller. This person, another Scottish lorry driver from the same area as the two men who had died, had evidently stopped at the scene of the accident and had taken it upon himself to pass on the tragic news as soon as he arrived home.

Unfortunately, this was during the early hours and certainly well before the local policeman got there, and of course I had no way of knowing how the awful news had been broken to this lady. Anyway, I suppose anger was just one of the emotions surfacing in the aftermath of such a tragic event, and it was probably understandable that this should be vented against the police. There was obviously not much I could do by way of consolation.

I never heard from this lady again, but later that same day I received two representatives of the transport firm that had lost the two employees in the accident, and I got them to do the formal identifications. One was fairly straightforward, as these things went, but the second body seemed to have borne the brunt of the 20-ton load of bricks the lorry was carrying when it hit the bridge. In this case, about all there was to identify was the collected contents of a plastic bag which had defeated even the cosmetic skills of our worthy mortuary attendant. The tough lorry men were visibly shaken as they left the mortuary.

These two fatal motorway accidents had happened while I was off duty, and I only came in at the tail-end of them, as it were. One 'fatal' that occurred on a minor road in the area rather sticks in my mind because I was concerned with the subsequent inquiry myself from start to finish and I knew some of the people involved. The story also had an unfortunate twist to it.

The driver of the car in this case was the son of a local businessman. In his early twenties, he had a fast car and his driving tended to exhibit all the signs of youthful exuberance. One night he was travelling with his teenage girlfriend on a country road when their car left the road on a slight bend and ended up in the ditch. Both young people were taken to hospital, where the unfortunate girl was found to be dead and the young man was detained for a short time with superficial injuries.

From the length of the tyre marks on the road surface and on the grass verge, it was apparent that a fair amount of speed had been involved here, but there were no independent witnesses and only the driver had survived to say what had happened. While I put a lot of effort into the inquiry, I had to suggest in my report that, despite the fatality, the evidence was insufficient to justify any charge other than driving without due care and attention. The papers went to a solicitor for his independent opinion, and he agreed with my recommendation as to proceedings. The lad entered a plea of guilty to the careless driving charge and the case was dealt with at the magistrates' court by way of a fine and licence endorsement.

Before the case came to court, I had a visit at the police station from the girl's father. Obviously grief-stricken at the loss of his only daughter, he was outraged that the person responsible for her death was only facing what he regarded as a minor driving charge. I explained that the charge was based on the available evidence which had been subjected to independent scrutiny. I added that I could not go into any detail at this stage but invited him to call back after the court proceedings were finalized, if he thought that might help.

I had every sympathy for this poor man but did not see him again. What particularly disturbed me was his conviction that 'that organisation' had fixed it for the lad to face the least possible charge. I knew he meant the 'Brotherhood' but I also knew I had done this particular inquiry myself and no untoward influences had been brought to bear on me (and would not have succeeded even if they had been). This man would have been aware that freemasonry was well represented in the police, including senior staff at this police station, and he may well have known, or believed, something relevant about the young driver's family. Anyway, this case brought it home to me that it was probably best for policemen not to be members of the esteemed Brotherhood, whatever its influence may be.

A fatal road accident is a horrifying human tragedy, and I sometimes thought society generally did not take the issue seriously enough. It was fashionable for well-meaning people to worry themselves about problems like emissions from Sellafield and the noise of low-flying aircraft in the Lake District while apparently ignoring the 100 a week death toll on UK roads at this time. We had even invented a silly expression like 'joy-riding' to trivialise the idiotic practice of tearing about in stolen cars.

Having said that, I hope it does not sound odd – and certainly not the least bit callous – if I say I did not mind dealing with fatal road accidents. After all, the thing had happened and there was nothing you could have done to prevent it, but it was up to you as a police officer to sort it out as best you could. In essence, I always saw it as a challenge to try and establish what had led up to the accident and also as a human problem in dealing with the people involved at the scene and in the aftermath. In particular, I was never aware of feeling any of the 'trauma' that you sometimes hear about from members of the emergency services dealing with these things.

If you were busy at the scene you did not have time to let your emotions get out of hand, and the real problems could come afterwards when you were trying to sort out all the paperwork. You may have spent an hour or two at the scene of the accident but it was likely to be a week or two before you got the file away off your desk. As in so many areas of policing, the challenge lay not so much 'on the ground' but rather in keeping the paperwork moving. Television drama about the police never shows this bit, but then it wouldn't because of course it has no entertainment value.

When I moved from force headquartes in 1977 to 'ordinary outside duty', as street patrol was called, it was about twelve years since I had been on regular beat duty. In the interval, apart from the spell as staff officer, I had had some years on traffic patrol, but this was rather different from the miscellany that was 'ordinary outside duty'. Some significant changes had occurred and I could not help making comparisons on a 'then and now' basis.

Cumbria Constabulary had more or less doubled in strength, about half the increase being accounted for by the fact that in 1974 we had taken over what had been a division of Lancashire Police together with a small part of Yorkshire. Before the local government re-organisation of that year we had five small territorial divisions based on the main towns, each headed by a superintendent, but now we had four larger divisions headed by chief superintendents. All the superintendents were still in place, now being in charge of sub-divisions instead of divisions, and all the chief superintendents and superintendents had deputies one rank below themselves.

In the divisions in the 1960s there had been a total of perhaps ten officers above the rank of inspector. With the 1974 changes, this figure had grown to around thirty. The picture was repeated at force HQ where the three main departments of administration, CID and traffic were now headed by chief superintendents instead of superintendents, and each chief superintendent had a deputy one rank below himself. CID and traffic department strengths had grown appreciably, and there had been developments in lesser specialist departments like training, planning and dogs.

We now had traffic wardens, and civilian staffs in general had grown apace, both at headquarters and in the divisions. Increased civilianization was supposed to release police officers to get on with their primary functions, but it was difficult to see where all the 'released' police officers had gone – unless it was to the specialist departments or to be promoted to complete the burgeoning rank structures beneath all the new-found chief superintendents.

I hasten to say that the changes in Cumbria were in line with what had been happening in other police forces throughout the country. We were no different from anybody else. The developments of course had been supported by the Police Authority and approved by the Home Office, which oversaw all changes in police establishments. The stated aim of these moves was to improve the quality of service to the public, and the individual member of the public must be left to decide for himself how far that objective was fulfilled.

The problem for anyone responsible for policing 'on the ground' was that he had an awful lot of probationers, while it had been put about by chief constables that the uniformed patrol officer was the 'backbone of the service'. This claim was no doubt based on a belief that it was what the public – or perhaps more to the point, politicians – wanted to hear. The reality was that by around 1970 the beat patrol staff was little more than a pool from which to fill vacancies as they arose in the specialised departments. The inevitable outcome was that beat patrol staffs tended to be composed of the very young and those who had either not managed to get themselves into a specialised department or, alternatively, had been kicked out of one.

In making these observations, I imply no criticism of the

personal qualities of most of the young people who made up the average town patrol staff. Many were admirable and did a surprisingly good job under pressure, despite their inexperience. The problem was that the distinct impression had been created in recent years that beat patrol was little more than an initial obstacle to be got out of the way before proceeding to some real police work in a specialised department like CID or traffic. We even saw Home Office-sponsored press adverts for well-motivated police recruits which suggested they could be chief inspectors within seven years.

It used to be said that it took ten years to learn to be a policeman. When I started in the job nobody was likely to make his first promotion before then – perhaps the change represented progress. I suppose it all depended on how much importance you attached to the police function, but I wondered how many people would have been happy to know that the person servicing their car or fixing their gas boiler had only a year or so of experience.

Every town police station had a communications centre, usually called the control room. The 999 system was likely to terminate there, along with VHF (forcewide) and UHF (local) radio and teleprinter, while fax and computer terminals were still to come at this time. I suppose you might call it the station nerve centre. There was often some argument about where in a police station the control room should be located, but at all except the largest stations it was likely to be near the public enquiry desk since control room staff would probably be required to deal with public callers as well. Ideally, no doubt, these two functions should have been separated, but this was unlikely to be justified by volume of work at the small to average station.

In my early days in the job at Kendal there was a pretty rudimentary VHF radio system in touch with the few traffic patrol cars that were likely to be out on the road at any one time. There was no UHF radio or teleprinter network (and the fax and computer systems were 20-odd years away).

My new station served a town only half the size of the old one, yet the control room usually seemed a much busier place than the earlier one had been. The VHF radio was a lot more active because there were now a lot more vehicles out on VHF, and the teleprinter was always rattling away with all sorts of stuff that was probably 95% irrelevant to us but had been circulated on a 'just in case' basis.

The technology that had produced the biggest change was the UHF personal radio system. When I started in the job you were out on your own on your feet with nobody but the public to call upon or talk to. It could be a bit lonely at times, and often you would hope that somebody would make you feel wanted by asking you the time or the way to Woolworths or something. Sometimes when all was quiet on your patrol you would wonder if any of your colleagues were having any more luck with a bit of excitement on theirs. Being on your own, you were aware of your limitations although you did grow into the role. You learned to use your initiative and your discretion a lot, but I suppose instinctively you thought you might get help from the public if you really needed it – if you went about things the right way.

The arrival of the UHF personal radio in the late 1960s represented the biggest-ever change to the beat man's job. All of a sudden he could talk to his base station at will and they could talk to him. Information about any incident that affected or seemed likely to affect more than one beat area of the town could be passed simultaneously to everyone. The constable was no longer on his own. If he needed help or information or guidance all he had to do was use his personal radio. Each town had its own UHF radio system with no more range than was appropriate for local coverage, but eventually technical advances made it possible for the central force HQ control to use the radio set-up to contact all beat patrols on duty throughout the county, if necessary.

Obviously, then, the personal radio was a major development in terms of organisational efficiency; yet there was bound to be a price to pay, and I am not sure the problems were always acknowledged. Naturally the personal radios were very expensive items of equipment that could sometimes give trouble. People were needed to maintain them, and the radio traffic they generated put more demand on the control centres. Probably the main potential problem area that was never really addressed was the human one – the effect on the outlook of the individual user of having this magic little device clipped to the front of his uniform. Would it affect his perception of his police powers or his relations with that awkward lot, the general public?

By this time also the foot patrols with the personal radios were supplemented by the sub-divisional van, a medium-sized multi-purpose vehicle with a crew of one or two that was always readily available in the town area. Unlike in the old days, quick response to incidents was virtually guaranteed. That must be a giant leap forward surely – in theory, certainly, but unfortunately not always in practice. The old-style policeman would tell you there was rarely anything to be gained by rushing to things. Why not take it quietly so as to arrive unflustered when the trouble might have simmered down a bit? Let the fire service or the ambulance rush to the scene if they wanted, but personally I could never see much merit in the police tearing about the place, either on foot or in a vehicle, and risking getting involved in an accident while speeding to an incident was worse than useless and too awful to contemplate.

The type of incident where I always thought haste on the part of the police was particularly counter-productive was the all-too-familiar late-night punch-up outside the pub or club. If a few young men with a skinful of drink want to knock hell out of each other, so what? It will probably be all over in a few minutes anyway without involving any innocent passer-by, so what is the sense of any policeman rushing into the middle of it? Yet it kept happening, with possible injuries to police, complaints against police, a big fat file for the Crown Prosecution Service and hours in court a couple of months later. All rather sordid, and it rarely did anything for the police image, perhaps most importantly in the eyes of the worthy magistrates who had to sit patiently listening to all the allegations and counter-allegations so long after the event.

Potentially even more embarrassing could be the call for 'backup'. The scenario I have in mind is the little band of midnight revellers with the cheeky one who shouts across the street at the keen young policeman on the other side, 'Black bastard!' Rising to the bait, and confident of support if needed, our black-clad figure would cross the street to remonstrate with Loudmouth, and things would start to go downhill from there. Outnumbered and starting to feel threatened, the constable takes it upon himself to exercise his power of arrest for drunk and disorderly or breach of the peace and presses the button on his personal radio to call up the van which he knows is not far away.

The two likely lads in the van understandably do not hang about when there is a colleague in trouble, and at the scene a couple of minutes later they find him struggling with Loudmouth, whose mates are trying to rescue him. Even bigger battle ensues and the rest is as per the foregoing paragraph – injuries, complaints, big file and hours in court. It is probably not the sort of thing the seekers after organisational efficiency had in mind when they thought of the personal radio, but it could and did happen – a lot.

In making these observations about the dangers of haste, let me emphasise once again that I am not criticising the personal qualities of the vast majority of the young people the police were getting as recruits. While you cannot put old heads on young shoulders, I am not sure the job in general was doing enough at this time to inculcate the advantages of restraint in day-to-day policing. Indeed, the organisation could put probationers under quite a bit of pressure to put in the paperwork – which of course meant making arrests and reporting offences – and at one point I felt obliged to take issue with a senior member of the force training department over his alleged tendency to ridicule probationers on his courses who were not producing the 'results' that suited him. Then again, it was becoming fashionable to talk about 'response times' to incidents, and this inevitably produced pressure for haste, often quite unnecessarily and sometimes with very unfortunate side-effects like assaults on police and damage to vehicles.

It was not just among the relatively inexperienced town patrol staff that this more aggressive style of policing was being adopted. Traffic patrols were greater in number than they had been in my early days in that department and they seemed to consider themselves under more pressure to achieve an impressive tally of reports for offences and particularly of arrests. This had its effect on the town police station because traffic department arrests were brought there as well; and some of these could be a shade borderline as far as weight of evidence was concerned, almost as if the traffic man concerned was thinking, 'Well, I've got my tick on the score sheet for this arrest and now it's up to this lot at the town police station to sort out the details.'

My own concern about this kind of attitude among the 'specialists' in the traffic department caused me one day to make a quick run out to the nearby M6 motorway exit road where a traffic car had stopped a southbound coach whose occupants were believed to have stolen a dartboard from a public house just over the Scottish border. My reaction was prompted by a fear that we would be swamped by the sudden arrival at the station of a coachload of football supporters on suspicion of theft or brought in for checking out or whatever. I got there just in time because the dartboard had been found on the coach and the traffic car crew were considering next steps in view of their failure to get a 'cough' from the culprit among the sea of faces on the vehicle.

Just then a Scottish police car arrived, about 25 miles off their area but fine as far as I was concerned. I gave the Scots lads 'their' dartboard and chased the football supporters. Everybody seemed happy except our traffic lads, who might just possibly have looked a little thwarted. Anyone who thinks it would not have happened might like to know that it would not have been the first time a coachload of people had been deposited at a police station en masse on suspicion of a minor offence by one of their number.

Of course, it has to be remembered that the late 1970s was a time when people generally – and especially young people – were getting used to being more assertive and challenging in all sorts of ways. We had had years of labour troubles culminating in the 'winter of discontent' and Arthur Scargill and his miners imposing their will by outnumbering the police. Organised labour had brought about the downfall of Edward Heath's government and given every appearance of dictating national policy through the Labour government that followed.

National affairs had been looking a bit chaotic at times, and no doubt it was inevitable that the police, as obvious symbols of authority, would not be finding life any easier at street level. Public order seemed to be becoming a problem area but we did not appear to be doing much planning for it – apart from the riot training, which might have been necessary but somehow looked a bit negative on its own.

So there were more public pressures on the police than there had been in the 1960s. For their part, the police had a lot more equipment, particularly vehicles and communications, that on the face of it should have enhanced organisational efficiency. Certainly we were reporting more offences and filling the cells more often, but was it really getting us anywhere? Were things getting any better for the increased police activity, or were we just in danger of going round in circles? Was it all worth it? Or was it just possible that the more the police claimed to be the 'professional' body to do something about society's ills, the more likely they were to be blamed for their inevitable failure? Did anybody care? Well, at least the police got some good pay rises out of it, and the 1978 Edmund-Davies formula was to keep police pay near the top of the league table right into the 1990s.

If a gap had opened up between the police and the public, Mr John Alderson in Devon and Cornwall had the answer: Community Policing. It was fashionable at this time to stick the word community in front of all kinds of public bodies, no doubt as a simple and inexpensive way of making them sound caring and committed. Why not Community Police to distinguish the nice ones from those who might lock you up? I even saw 'Community Police' written on vehicles in Cornwall and thought that was taking it a bit far, but maybe my sense of humour was lacking.

On a more serious note, I could not help thinking our moves towards organisational efficiency – the vehicles, the communications systems, the specialisation and so on – were in danger of taking us farther away from the public. There is never likely to be a totally easy relationship between police and public, however much we may like to pretend there should be, but perhaps we were trying to be too 'professional', at the expense of our relations with the public 'on the ground'. We might even have been starting to give the impression to the public that 'we can manage without you, thank you very much.'

A minor, but perhaps significant, example of this attitude must be the police tendency to issue press statements about serious crime suspects with the added warning that 'the public should not approach him'. This is ridiculous: it is everybody's civic duty to try and prevent crime and apprehend offenders, not just a police job. Anybody whose memory goes back to before 1980 will recall the case where a particularly vicious murder suspect known as the 'Black Panther' was grabbed by two miners in Nottingham – and no doubt they were just the lads to do it.

By 1980 Cumbria had a new chief constable to succeed the celebrated autocrat who had retired. For what it was worth, I felt a bit uneasy about early local press features on the new man, extolling his culinary skills and picturing him brandishing his pots and pans. First impressions do count, as they say, and as an ex-Metropolitan Police man, he might have been well advised that Cumbrians do not necessarily appreciate self-publicity of that kind.

Later on that year I was off duty in the bar of the club at police headquarters when I was approached informally by the deputy chief constable, who asked if I would be interested in a move back to force HQ. After my earlier comments about headquarters it might be supposed that I would have declined the offer but that really was not a practical proposition. After all, I had been given the opportunity by the deputy chief constable to stay on at HQ when my move out was first mooted nearly four years earlier, and about a year after that the possibility had arisen of a return to headquarters.

On that occasion I had asked to remain in the sub-division

a bit longer and this had been agreed by the deputy chief constable with all the usual consideration he had always shown to me personally. So I really could not have turned down this chance even if I had wanted to, but in any case I had been long enough in my current role and felt it was time to move on. Being quite pleased to be asked, I thought it might have seemed a bit churlish to look for details of what the deputy chief constable had in mind, and no more was said about it.

6
PROJECT TEAM

It was December 1980 when I got a call to police headquarters to meet the new assistant chief constable. He had transferred to us recently from another northern police force and this was the first time I had met him. He turned out to be a man of about my own age or perhaps rather younger who impressed as a forthright sort of individual.

The assistant chief constable said it had been decided to form a 'Project Team' to plan the development of a major communications/computer project. This was to be based on a review of force organisation from an operational point of view. Cumbria Police's communications systems needed updating, he said, and the question of computerisation was to be central to the whole thing. He asked if I was interested in joining the project team. I was rather taken by surprise, despite the brief conversation I had had with the deputy chief a few weeks earlier about a possible move to headquarters. The assistant chief constable noticed my hesitation in replying and before I could say anything he added, 'We're not looking for a "yes" man. This is a big new project, and we have to get it right first time. This is a team effort and everybody will have his contribution to make. We're particularly looking for somebody who'll say, "hang on a minute", if we seem to be going too fast.'

Old police hands might think that last point was a bit of a leg-pull but this project team thing was something new to Cumbria (as of course was the assistant chief constable and also the chief constable himself). Anyway, my previous police experience had apparently been taken into account in choosing me for this particular job along with things like my

Police College report of four years earlier. It would be about a three-year commitment.

I asked for time to think about it, and this was agreed. I left police headquarters that day with very mixed feelings. I was now in my 40s, with eighteen years' police service, and I had to accept that a glowing future in the job was unlikely, but I did not want to stay on general police duty for the rest of my service. Rightly or wrongly, I prided myself on my organising and planning ability, and quite obviously this project was a major exercise in that particular field. On the other hand, while a communications update might be on the cards, the emphasis on the acquisition of an operational computer system surprised me because with all my police service in this mainly rural county of ours it had never occurred to me that we were desperately in need of a computer handling day-to-day police functions.

I knew the county council computer worked out pay and allowances for the 1500 or so of us on the police payroll and I was entirely satisfied with its performance, but I took it that all it really had to be was a fast adding machine. Then again, if the council computer now and again had a bit of 'down-time' (computer-speak for conking out or needing attention), that surely could not be too critical because it did not have to keep working round the clock.

A computer in the police control function seemed to me to be a different matter altogether. Obviously it would have to deal with incidents as they happened, on a 24-hour basis and with a high degree of reliability. And it would hardly be doing the same basic task from month to month with the same operators but rather the miscellany of mainly minor matters that was policing, with all sorts of different operators.

These early thoughts about the proposed computer system were more of an instinctive reaction than a studied one because I had never before had cause to give the implications any particular thought. At the same time, the impression I had was that this particular project was being taken seriously, and any drawbacks would surely emerge in the planning stage as well as the likely benefits. I was particularly mindful of what the new assistant chief constable had said about the need for a cautious approach to the exercise. I thought that sounded eminently sensible in such unknown territory and believed there must be a role for me in this. I realised I had to take it.

At this stage my understanding of what was proposed was that there would be computer terminals (i.e. keyboard and screen) at each of the force control rooms. We had a control room at force headquarters and a control at each of the six sub-divisional headquarters stations. Headquarters control, which had a staff of about six on duty at any one time, handled all the traffic patrol cars, the 70-mile stretch of the M6 motorway and major incidents throughout the county. The other controls dealt with day-to-day matters within their own areas, and most of them had a staff of about two (one police officer and one 'civilian'). In the sub-divisions the controller's job was a miscellaneous one, in the sense that it was not only a matter of handling incidents on the telephone and radio systems but also of looking after the station telephone switchboard, attending to public callers at the counter and making regular visits to any prisoners in the cells.

The controller's job nevertheless was a responsible one, and in the sub-divisions it was normally given to the most experienced constable on the town patrol shift. He usually had his civilian assistant readily available and he could call on supervisory help (sergeant or inspector) if necessary. As usual in the police force, workload could vary between quiet and hectic with rarely a happy medium.

Incidents needing police attention were recorded by control room operators on a standard message form, along with details of the police response and other relevant actions until the matter was finalised from a control point of view. The purpose was to maintain a record of what had happened and what was done about it, in as concise a form as possible. Such incident logs were handwritten or typed by the control operator concerned and filed away together on a daily basis, for future reference if necessary.

As I understood it, what was envisaged with the computer system was that a visual display unit (VDU) screen and keyboard would replace the paper records of incidents needing police attention. The operator would enter details of the occurrence on the screen, and entry of the appropriate police beat code would then display the 'resources' (police patrols) in the area that were available to deal with it. Once someone was sent to the scene, all relevant actions to deal with the incident would be entered into the computer at the time and displayed on the screen. Of course, there was more to it than that but that was the basis of it.

Anyway, with scant knowledge of computers at this stage, on 5 January 1981 I emptied my desk at the town police station and reported to my new job at force HQ. There were four other police members of the project team at the outset. A chief inspector and a very young policewoman had already been doing some groundwork for a year or so, and they were to remain as members of the newly constituted team. The other two members were a sergeant and a constable who were taking up their new jobs in the ranks of temporary inspector and temporary sergeant respectively. Two non-police computer people were to join us a month or two later.

On taking up this new challenge, I was immediately conscious of the huge scale of the project and its likely revolutionary impact on the organisation of a small police force that had evolved over decades to meet the perceived needs of an essentially rural area. Without wanting to feel like grandad, I was also conscious of my age and experience, both inside and outside the job, in relation to my new-found colleagues, all of whom were ex-cadets apart from the temporary inspector.

Their average age was 30-ish and average length of service around ten years, but quite frankly the project team leader represented the biggest area of concern as far as I was concerned. Endowed as he was with all the attributes of an ex-police cadet and long insulated from exposure to the outside world's corrupting influences, it was to the team leader's eternal credit that he had managed to garner the fruits of all the recent incoming mail about police computing that had confused or repelled less prescient colleagues at police HQ. With a new chief constable who knew nothing about Cumbria but wanted a computer system come what may – like many of his forward-thinking counterparts in other areas – the eagerly enthusiastic team leader seemed to believe the time was ripe for a big leap forward.

What mainly struck me, however, among initial reactions was the overwhelming need for care in planning such a major development if the effort and expense involved was to be justified by results. We faced a three-year task and there was talk of costs of the order of £1 million. I had never tackled anything on such a scale, and I knew my new-found colleagues hadn't either.

Shortly after returning to force headquarters, I learned that all inspectors with more than a couple of years' service in the rank could apply for a career management interview before the chief constable and deputy chief constable. Having just given a commitment in effect to stay where I was for the next three years or so, I wondered at first if there was any point in applying but nevertheless decided it might be best if I did.

My interview was fixed for 4pm one day in early March at police headquarters. I duly presented myself in best uniform at the chief constable's secretary's office on the top landing at 3.50pm, hoping there would be no delay because the building – or this part of it at least – was very warm and I was in full uniform including a rather heavy jacket. Nothing happened for over half an hour. Not only was I physically uncomfortable because of the heat but it occurred to me that the two exalted interviewers had seen a lot of my other colleagues that day already and probably would be getting tired of the process by this time.

I had never met the chief, who had been with us for just a matter of months, and his view of me would inevitably be based on whatever papers about me he had in front of him. Someone had no doubt done a report about me in preparation for this interview but I had never seen or heard mention of it and did not even know who had done it. I had over eighteen years' service but had no means of knowing the accuracy or otherwise of my personnel record. It may all sound a bit quaint but this was the police force after all.

At 4.30pm I was called into the chief's office. He was sitting behind his large desk and very much in the middle of it while the deputy chief was perched rather awkwardly off to the left. It was almost as if – perish the thought – the chief was intent on emphasising his own supremacy while putting his deputy at an obvious disadvantage. I took the single chair in the middle of the floor facing the desk.

The chief opened the proceedings. He did not mention the delay but got straight down to business. Looking down at the papers on his desk, he said by way of openers, 'Six years on motorcycle patrol? What on earth does that mean?' While not quite appreciating the reasoning behind the supplementary question, I replied, 'Well, sir, I was on motorcycle patrol back in the 60s but it was for nothing like six years.

Perhaps one or two but even that was not full-time, particularly in the later stages.'

My record of postings turned out to be totally inaccurate. As I discovered subsequently, there were several important issues simply missed out; and there was no mention, for example, of the successes I had had all those years ago on traffic patrol or the then chief constable's congratulations to me at the time. (Having discovered the omissions from my record, it took a fair bit of persistence on my part to get something done about it, but of course the damage was done for now).

The chief threw another one at me from these nebulous papers on his desk: 'Your wife runs an old people's home? You must be better paid than a chief constable!' I hoped my sense of humour was not failing me but did not find it easy to answer that one. I glanced over at the deputy. He looked a bit uncomfortable. Well, he was only a deputy chief constable.

The chief looked up from his papers and said, 'I believe you are supposed to be a hard-headed man on a young and enthusiastic team.' The tone was just a touch sardonic. Taking it at face value, however, I was not sure about the strict accuracy of the chief's description of either myself or the team but did feel moved to suggest that the comment implied a very demanding role in view of the nature of the police force and the three-year timescale of the project. The chief went on to say that the object of the computer system was efficiency through release of police staff for ordinary outside duty. Ever the thinker, I could not help wondering whether that ideal would be achieved through what we were setting out to do.

After ten minutes or so of this sort of professional profundity from the chief constable, it was the deputy's turn to have his say. He had been sitting quietly up to now, looking rather uncomfortable in his slightly off-set chair that was naturally rather smaller than the chief's (all good management stuff, this), but he went straight on the offensive. His line of questioning was characteristically aggressive in tone, although I cannot now remember anything of the content. I am not sure what that implies but think I was a touch sad about it at the time because it was so pointless, he and I being so well known to each other.

Then it was back to the chief. He just started to say something when the 'phone rang. He picked it up and gave the caller his undivided attention for a minute or so. I glanced at my watch. It was now after 5pm. The chief said, 'Yes, right,' and put the 'phone down. Maybe it was his good lady and he was late for his tea. Anyway, he lost interest in the proceedings and the interview was quickly terminated. I left the wood-panelled and book-lined inner sanctum thinking it had been over half an hour since I went in but, by Jove, how time flies when you are enjoying yourself.

I was not sure what purpose this meeting had served for any of the three middle-aged men involved. I could not think what I was supposed to have learned from it. I did not get any subsequent counselling/de-brief or whatever, any more than there had been any discussion with anyone about it beforehand. Still, this was the police force after all: if you can't take a joke you shouldn't have joined, as they used to say. However, I happened to meet the deputy chief constable in the yard at police HQ a couple of days later. He was of course the man I had known virtually since joining the job and the deputy chief I had worked for as staff officer for five years not all that long ago. He must have felt he owed me a comment about the interview as he said, 'I thought you acquitted yourself well. You were right not to just let that 'hard-headed' bit pass. Oh, and it was my job to take the aggressive line.'

He walked on, and I reflected on what he had said. His first sentence suggested the chief might have thought something different about the interview but he was no 'yes' man to this newcomer (the chief), was he? The 'hard-headed' bit would really only have originated with the deputy himself and the chief was probably trying to use it to take the mickey out of him as well as me. As for the last point the deputy made, it sounded as if he had been watching too many of those TV cop programmes where the two detectives try to wrong-foot their suspect with their alternating Mr Nice Guy/Mr Nasty technique.

So a bit of stock-taking would not go amiss – I had nearly 20 years' service, was in my 40s and had held the rank of inspector for seven years. I had joined the police in my mid-20s after some varied experience outside and had always taken the job seriously. Without complacency I hope, I thought I had been fairly successful in what I had done and seemed up to now to have been well regarded by people in authority.

By nature, I had sometimes been inclined to question (with honourable motives) when acceptance might have been more prudent. Despite that (or perhaps even because of it), I had been promoted twice by the time I had eleven years' service; but even that rapid advancement had taken me to my late 30s, an age at which the real highflyers in this modern police service of ours could expect to be at the rank of at least chief superintendent after joining at the age of 20 or so. Our new assistant chief constable, for instance, was only fortyish after joining from cadet service at nineteen.

While I felt more comfortable making the decisions than taking the orders, I suppose I would not always have been seen to show quite the single-minded ambition that some others did; and experience dictated that if you did not use the system then it would use you. Still, while I could hardly look forward to a glowing future in the job, I wanted to continue to put my best efforts into it on the basis that you only get out what you put in.

Back with the project team, we had started with a short computer planning course from people with experience of these matters. I was heartened to learn that the recognised essential first step in such an exercise was the preparation of a feasibility study. This seemed entirely logical. It had been decided, though, that we would dispense with that stage in the interests of rapid progress! I was horrified. To me, it was like starting to build a house without bothering with a plan or putting in the foundations.

Instead, we spent the first couple of months preparing what was called an organisational review. This covered current working methods under all sorts of headings, particularly from a control point of view, and sought to highlight any apparent problems. In each case only computer solutions were proposed without much consideration of the steps necessary to achieve those aims.

The organisational review was put out as a consultative document and given wide circulation throughout the Cumbria force. Comment was invited on the radical proposals it contained, but there were no comments at all – none whatsoever – the silence was deafening.

Surely there must have been some opinions out there about this giant leap forward, but nobody was going to commit himself to a reasoned comment in writing, favourable or otherwise. The problem was highlighted for me one afternoon just after publication of the organisational review, when I happened to be in a divisional control room far from police HQ. It was around shift change-over time and there were quite a lot of uniformed figures about. Suddenly in swept the local chief superintendent with retinue, and he proceeded to attack me as a representative of an over-blown headquarters team that proposed to down-grade one of his sub-divisional controls. No doubt he had picked his time carefully to demonstrate his territorial loyalties to the maximum number of his staff who would spread the word that their chief super was not a man to be trifled with. I suggested he should put his argument officially to the appropriate quarters. Nothing more was heard from him.

Taking the total silence from the rest of the force as complete agreement with all the computer solutions set out in the organisational review, our next step as a team was to plunge straight into the preparation of a sizeable document known as an operational requirement. This outlined our computer requirements for circulation to commercial firms who might be interested in supplying us.

The move into computers was a recent one for police forces generally and quite new to us in Cumbria. As a team, we had made visits to two or three other police forces with operational computer systems; but the value of these trips seemed questionable, to say the least, because of a lack of before/after evaluation and the fact that these other forces had adopted different systems of policing from ours in Cumbria, involving far fewer police stations and much less public contact.

In Cumbria we had over 100 police stations, including many single-manned ones in the villages, while Bedfordshire for example (a force similar in size to us), had a total of only six. Apparently they had closed down most of their rural police stations some years earlier and concentrated all their staff at the main centres of population. I pass no comment on the question whether this was good for policing generally in the county, but it must have made the move into computers a lot easier because of the much simpler force organisation and larger pools of staff available to operate the computer terminals at the control centres.

At this time Cumbria Police might have looked a bit old-fashioned compared to some, but with all my experience of this unique county of ours I could not help feeling we were probably not too far away from what the public wanted of us. I suppose it all depended on whether you thought the public – our 'customers' – really knew what they wanted. Of course, in our case members of the force had been consulted on our computer proposals with the result set out above. There had been no public soundings, although the County Police Committee had given the go-ahead on expenditure.

The fact was that none of us had any experience of computers, and yet we were proposing to use a large amount of public money to introduce a very complex computer system into a largely rural force that had expressed no interest in it whatsoever. It would not have been so bad if we had been going for a simple system without a lot of applications on it, but we were expecting it to do all sorts of things in the hands of operators who were yet to be identified and trained. It seemed a bit like a man without any knowledge of cars going to the manufacturers and asking them to develop him a vehicle to his own vague specification in the hope that it would run and that he would be able to drive it (but thinking that in any case it should impress the neighbours).

We were not proposing to introduce a computer system that had been in use in another police force. That would not have worked because each police force had its own sort of organisation to suit local needs. There would not have been much point in trying to bring a system from say, urban Manchester to rural Cumbria, and even apparently similar police areas could be run on very different lines, as in the case of Bedfordshire already mentioned.

So, with no feasibility study and an internal consultation process that had come to nothing, we were ready within a few short months to go to the manufacturers with our requirements. I found it all a bit hard to understand, but maybe I was just dimmer than everyone else.

We held regular team meetings at which these concerns were expressed but pressed on regardless. A technical adviser from the Home Office attended on a regular basis and he seemed to be not over-confident about what we were doing, although his contribution was minimal. Of course, it has to be borne in mind that the Home Office could not give directions to police forces, but our man seemed to have no more than a watching brief. Perhaps he could not understand the Cumbrian accents!

He listened carefully to an outline of my thoughts about our unseemly haste at a private conversation I had with him but all he could suggest was that I should record these matters on paper. With the greatest respect to him, I had already done that but of course I was on my own with it. Being in the early stages of their police careers, my youthful teammates in this exercise had naturally been chosen not only for their undoubted intelligence but also for their inevitable acquiescence in whatever was officially proposed. That was how the police force was, however much you talked about the team concept with everyone having his say.

I documented discussions we had during the next few months about issues that looked important to me. I suppose by now I did not really expect too much but still felt I had to try. Perhaps harking back to what the chief constable had said at the recent interview about the computer releasing police staff for ordinary outside duty, I submitted a paper outlining some views about likely demands on control operators in the proposed computer system and suggesting the need for some thinking about basic issues that had not been covered.

The day after the paper was submitted, I was called up to

the assistant chief constable's office and got a frosty reception:

Assistant chief constable: 'Do you want to remain a member of the team?'

Taken aback, I replied, 'I did not know that was an issue. What is the problem?'

Assistant chief constable: 'This paper about the controls. Policy decisions have been made and they have got to go ahead.'

I did not have a copy of the paper with me but was sure I had not been querying any policy decisions. Having just spent four years at one of the proposed control centres to be affected by the computer system, I felt qualified to know what the operators currently did and thought we were making light of the changes the computer must bring to the job. The purpose of the paper was to suggest that we should now be giving some more consideration to what would be expected of the computer operators. Wanting no argument with our esteemed assistant chief constable, I explained what I had been trying to do and added that it seemed quite natural for me to raise an issue of this kind that I was concerned about.

The assistant chief constable replied, 'Yes, and it's very creditable, but we have a tight time scale. This is holding things up!' After a moment's thought, I saw no way out of reminding the assistant chief constable what he had told me only a few months before when he asked me to do this job; that is, that they wanted someone on the team with the ability to say, 'Hang on a minute', if things seemed to be moving too fast. I added that the chief constable had said much the same thing shortly afterwards when he referred to the otherwise 'young and enthusiastic team'.

The assistant chief constable looked at the floor and went silent. With all due deference to his rank, I had no wish to have the last word but felt obliged to break the silence by pointing out that my action in urging caution at this stage would have been just the same even if he and the chief had not told me what they did, because caution and commonsense were things I prided myself on anyway. Still, I expressed my regret for any misunderstanding arising out of the paper I had submitted.

On leaving, I reflected on the fact that I had not been in the assistant chief constable's office since that day around nine months earlier when he asked me to join the project team, and he had not given any hint of dissatisfaction with what I had done in the meantime. However, the atmosphere in his office had been such that I had no doubt this little confrontation had been the culmination of an assiduous attempt to have me shifted off the project team. I refreshed my memory on the contents of the paper in question but could not see anything in it that looked at all subversive. It was in effect intended to document an item at a team discussion we had had.

I went back to our team quarters and asked our leader why he had taken the paper to the assistant chief constable without telling me. He said I was 'holding up the project'. I thought that caution was vital to the interests of the force but that hitherto I had completely failed to make any impact in that respect!

From the start I had got the distinct impression that our team leader had not exactly welcomed my presence on his outfit. Being appreciably older than the others (and him also for that matter), I probably seemed to be something of a challenge to his authority, and apparently he had had a say in the appointment of all the team members except me. Clearly he had been doing his best to solve the problem. The reasons then started to come out. While I had known this gentleman for some years, I was taken aback by the concerns he had been harbouring. He said in effect that the deputy chief constable, who had treated him with contempt in the past and was opposed to the computer project, had briefed me to put obstacles in his way!

I emphasised that the deputy chief constable had never mentioned the computer project to me. Our leader clearly did not believe me, although I could see no logical reason why he should think I would concoct a lie for his benefit. Clearly, there had been some serious misunderstandings and it was not certain that they had all been resolved by these discussions. There was no point in my going back to the assistant chief constable because he must have accepted the allegations put to him by our team leader, even though he had never discussed the situation with me before questioning my continued presence on the project team. There was certainly nothing to be gained by going to anyone higher than the assistant chief constable.

Obviously it was time to consider my position. I could have asked to be taken off the project team, but in the current circumstances I would not have been given a brilliant alternative posting. I do not think I seriously considered leaving the police because I still had a lot of time for the job (even though some of the influences within it now were not quite what I had been used to in the past), and I really could not see anything else I would have wanted to do at the time. In any case I was not going to leave the job until I was ready to do so.

Let us be clear about one thing: I was not blameless in this because I had been too idealistic in police terms and had not watched my back. I thought we were moving far too fast at this important planning stage and had recorded my concerns on paper along with what I thought were constructive suggestions. But any apparent questioning of methods, however well-intentioned, may be misunderstood by people conditioned by the police force from a very early age to see any 'non-conformity' as disruptive. The guiding principle has to be 'What's in it for me?'

Still, life had to go on. A computer handling the control functions was something fairly recent in the police service generally, and those forces that had taken that route usually seemed to have set out their requirements in a very detailed specification to potential suppliers. We were adopting a different approach. Over the next few months we provided a number of computer firms with a document which set out our requirements in quite general terms, in the belief that the computer people who were interested would use their technical expertise to come back to us with detailed proposals.

We could then choose what seemed to be the best one but use any interesting elements of the others to 'firm up' our final specification with the successful supplier. The theory was that this would allow us to draw on the experience of the professional computer people and also save time by avoiding the need for us to prepare a detailed technical specification.

By mid-1982 we had tenders for the computer installation from half a dozen potential suppliers. One quotation initially was appreciably lower than the others, but then one of the others had a major re-think on pricing and was eventually awarded the contract. This firm was soon beginning a planned one-year contract which in fact took more than two years to complete, despite seemingly exhausting efforts by all members of their young project team.

Early on in the contract, I understood the company's managing director left, along with the director of police projects. However, I am happy to say that the firm did eventually finish the job, and they had my admiration for that. Whether they did it within their fixed contract price I know not, although one's thoughts on this point were bound to be influenced by knowledge of the marked reduction in their quotation at the outset and their grossly over-optimistic estimate of timescale. What had happened, of course, was that the firm had taken on this contract on what were effectively our terms, in the expectation of getting a foothold in what they saw as the prestigious and lucrative market of police computing. Surely the risks must have been obvious and yet they had signed in the hope of gaining repeat contracts. It was to be hoped their strategy paid off.

The problems for software firms of fixed-price contracting for police computer systems was outlined in a technical journal of the time. The journal appeared to get near to the root of the problem in its appreciation of the fundamental point that each police force was an independent entity. Even if any police force embarking on computerisation really knew what it wanted, it would hardly take on a system developed for another police force because it would see itself as being different from all the others. I would have thought this would have been obvious to any computer firm taking any more than a cursory look at the nature of policing.

However, *tempus fugit* as they say; nearing the end of 1983 and completion of the computer assignment, it was time to reflect on the trials and tribulations of the last three years and take an interest in what life in the police force had in store. After that unresolved little, er, misunderstanding at the start of the computer project, I had dutifully switched off the thinking part of my persona that had seemed to be appreciated in the first eighteen years of my police service and merged into the 'young and enthusiastic' team around me.

I could not get a decision on what I was supposed to do next but at least things seemed to be ending on a reasonable note. I was not aware of any criticism of what I had done apart from that made of the paper I submitted in the early stages; and indeed as our assignment was drawing to a close

I was quite pleased to be commended in writing by the assistant chief constable for quality of work on various aspects of the project.

A few months later I was seconded to the force Research and Planning Department to set up a grandiose-sounding resource and establishment study. Cumbria, like every other police force no doubt, thought it needed more staff, but the Home Office would not authorise any increase in establishment without evidence that the existing workforce was fully occupied. That might seem reasonable enough on the face of it, but how do you measure police productivity – number of arrests made or traffic summonses issued or crimes prevented or what?

The solution was that every member of the force up to the rank of sergeant would be issued with a specially designed booklet (in addition to his pocket book) in which he would detail all aspects of his daily activities on duty over a set period of several months. The results would be fed into a computer and analysed to show what percentage of the force's time was spent on each of the various specified activities such as dealing with crime, road accidents, paperwork and so on. Actually, so much detail was asked for in the booklet – which had not been designed by me, I hasten to say – that it was bound to take a conscientious member an appreciable time every day to fill it in, to the extent that I thought there should have been an additional box on it to show 'Time taken to complete this document'.

Having just got the exercise off the ground, with the assistance of a worthy sergeant but without much relish, I was saved from further involvement in it by no less a personage than Mr Arthur Scargill of the National Union of Mineworkers.

Mr Scargill, it may be remembered, first came to prominence in the early 1970s when he and his massed pickets forced the closure of the Saltley coke depot in Birmingham, and the outnumbered local police were powerless to stop him. It seems that 1984 was to be his finest hour, but the differences this time included the fact that Mrs Thatcher was the incumbent of Number 10, not Mr Edward Heath, and there were massive coal reserves already on the ground. Of equal significance for anyone proposing massed 'industrial action' was the planning that had been done by the police in the interim to counter large-scale public disorder. A lot of effort had been going into organised public order training, and arrangements had been formalised for providing speedy police reinforcements for any force in difficulty with an event that seemed likely to get out of control.

As the 1984 coal strike built up, the National Reporting Centre (NRC) was activated at New Scotland Yard, and individual police forces needing help could telephone their requirements to the centre, which then had the job of drumming up the necessary reinforcements from other forces who could spare the staff. The basic unit for this sort of mutual aid was the Police Support Unit consisting of an inspector, two sergeants and 20 constables.

Naturally those police forces with the biggest number of coal mines in their areas were the ones most likely to contact the NRC for help during the strike, and the assistance would be required from other forces without current problems in that respect. Cumbria used to have a lot of coal mines but by the 1980s they had all closed so during the strike we often found ourselves at the receiving end of NRC requests for police support units at fairly short notice. Sometimes we had several police support units away from the county, in Yorkshire or wherever, at any one time so it was quite a drain on a fairly small force like ours.

In these circumstances it was pointless trying to do a resource and establishment study, which would have to reflect normal policing demands if it was to have any value at all, so the thing had to be postponed indefinitely. Instead I found myself taking the calls from the NRC, setting the wheels in motion to get together the police support units required, and arranging transport and other matters related to this long-running industrial dispute.

Incidentally, the NRC at this time often seemed to be portrayed in the press as a sinister set-up that was under direct political control from Number 10 or the Home Office. I only saw the centre as a temporary clearing house with police staff of about my own rank whose job it was to co-ordinate requests for assistance between police forces. Problems arising out of the strike were cropping up in various parts of the country simultaneously, and it would have been impossible to co-ordinate an effective police response involving large numbers of staff without a central reference point. The NRC seemed to fill that role quite well, and it was closed down when no longer required.

No, there was nothing sinister about the NRC, but whether the police image in general was improved during the miners' strike was another matter. Unlike the military, a police force usually seems to find its best expression through exercise of individual responsibility. Police in large numbers are not always the easiest people to keep control of, and any individual breaking ranks is likely to be the subject of immediate attention by the news media.

Various stories about police aberrations circulated during the 1984 strike, frequently arising out of the large amounts of paid overtime coming the way of individuals who often managed to get themselves assigned to police support units sent to other force areas. Some policemen, it was said, were inclined to provoke the strikers by waving £10 notes at them, and Arthur himself was supposed to be getting a lot of holiday postcards from policemen relaxing in faraway places who wanted to thank him for providing them with the necessary funds. One police contingent from a large force which went to help a Midlands force with a strike-related problem was said to have left with a selection of items from the silverware in the host force's Mess! An enterprising inspector in one northern force apparently was more inclined to include in police support units people who first showed their motivation by slipping him a bottle of whisky.

Towards the end of 1984 I was still officially a member of the computer project team but had had no actual involvement with it for over six months. I had not been officially transferred to the planning department but only seconded there for a particular task that had to be abandoned because of the miners' strike, which was not going to go on for ever. I felt a bit like Yosser Hughes, the Liverpool lad in the television drama who went about saying 'Gizza job!' Friends in the job were inclined to refer to me as the Minister without Portfolio, which I suppose was fair enough in the circumstances.

Seemingly I was *persona non grata* as far as the powers that be were concerned. Of course, in the police service if you really wanted to undermine anyone your best plan was to give him nothing to do. The organisation was not answerable to anyone for the use it was making of individual members of staff. Obviously it was depressing but it was essential to keep going and look undaunted, while looking out for something to get my teeth into.

The opportunity I had been seeking presented itself eventually when I got myself attached to a working party that was overseeing a major project based on the local town police station.

In the late 1970s a high-powered Royal Commission had been appointed to carry out a wide-ranging review of criminal procedure, and the recommendations in their report had led eventually to the Police and Criminal Evidence Act 1984. This Act was effectively all about police accountability and was to bring about major changes in police practices, particularly in the important areas of searches of persons and property, questioning and treatment of people in police custody and handling of complaints against police.

While the Act was not yet in force, it soon would be and it was clear that the part of it that related to treatment of detained persons would have major implications for police 'on the ground'. National guidelines had been produced in the form of a draft code of practice for dealing with detainees, and the Association of Chief Police Officers had obtained Home Office approval to carry out field trials in selected police areas. Cumbria was one of three police forces chosen to host the experiments, so we were to treat the code of practice as if it were already in force at one of our main police stations and see what problems it produced in handling detained persons in accordance with its provisions over a three-month period.

Suitable guidance was given to police staff at the local town station and surrounding sub-division (the guidance given being somewhat limited by our own still meagre understanding of all these new provisions), then we on the working party supervised what happened and acted as consultants where necessary. Afterwards we were responsible for producing a detailed report on our findings which achieved wide circulation nationally.

While previous experience had led me to be rather sceptical about apparent Home Office inertia, I was quite pleased this time to find that we gained agreement from them to make various changes to the draft code of practice we had been using. Our report about our field trials was also well received by other police forces that had not had the benefit of the experience we had had with the new arrangements.

This early practical experience of the Police and Criminal Evidence Act (PACE Act as it came to be called) and the code of practice convinced me that what we had here was a major piece of legislation whose significance for us was not yet fully appreciated by the police service at large. Accordingly, in January 1985 I submitted a report to the effect that the PACE Act would have major planning implications that needed urgent attention if we were to meet the 1 January 1986 deadline that had been set for implementation of all the Act's provisions.

The superintendent in charge of the Planning Department agreed with my assessment of the problem and sent my report on 'upstairs' with a suitable recommendation. We got no response, not even an acknowledgement, and the same thing happened to a couple of other reports on similar lines that we put up over the next two months. I was beginning to get used to being ignored so I was not unduly surprised by this lack of interest in my views, but at the same time I could see we were going to have our work cut out with this deadline less than a year away so I just got on with preparatory work anyway.

Suddenly, three months after my PACE Act reports began going in, it all started happening. My existence seemed to be acknowledged again. I was assigned to PACE Act planning full-time, as a matter or urgency, and was authorised to select any constable I thought suitable to assist me. After careful thought and sounding out the views of the individual concerned, I asked for the services of a mature male constable I had known for some years. Almost immediately I was sent a young female constable who was virtually unknown to me. With no disrespect to the young lady in question, I had probably got her because she was not wanted at her previous station, but you have to be philosophical about these things, don't you? Anyway, her personal qualities were admirable and I had no complaints about her.

Having spent several months with this sizable new Act – over 100 sections and far bigger than any previous Act of its kind – I was in no doubt that it would involve major changes in our ways of doing things and oblige us to throw away a significant part of our Force Orders. The emphasis on accountability would mean keeping all sorts of new records, and that would involve designing and introducing many new forms and documents, whether we liked it or not.

The fundamental problem I faced was that, while I thought I now knew a fair bit about this Act, the people who would have to make all the policy decisions arising out of it knew virtually nothing about it – and their interest could be deduced from the response I had been getting to my previous requests for attention to it.

The only solution I could see was that I would have to go through the whole Act, section by section, and 'translate' its legal jargon into relatively digestible English, at the same time highlighting the points where policy decisions would be required from my betters. This eventually resulted in a 30-page chart that I developed and presented in stages at monthly meetings of a PACE Act Policy Group chaired by the deputy chief constable. By this process I got all the decisions I wanted over the next few months, and was then able to finalise the six new Force Orders that were needed and the forty or so new or amended forms that the Act required.

On the way I had to motivate all sorts of people within our organisation and maintain contact with other bodies such as the Home Office and the Law Society. I was pleased also to be able to help people doing a similar job in other police forces who had not had the early advantage we had seen with the recent field trials. Anyway, the job was done and the results of my labours were circulated to all affected police stations in the county by December 1985, just in time for the Act becoming law on 1 January 1986.

I mention the preparations for this new Act because it may be that not everyone would realise the police had to do this sort of thing themselves, and each police force independently at that. There was no central body like the Home Office to do it for police forces, and it was not a lawyer's job. PACE Act was all about day-to-day policing and its effects on the public, and only a policeman with practical experience of the job could have sorted it out for the benefit of staff 'on the ground.'

I hope I do not sound self-congratulatory in talking about this Act. Being all about practical issues, it was an interesting project in its own right, but for me it was rather more than that. Having had something of a raw deal over the computer planning, I could see no way of putting my case in the aftermath other than by getting hold of a major challenge, like PACE Act, and sorting it out successfully. I thought I had done that. The chief constable himself congratulated me on what I had done, and I was particularly pleased to get no complaints from the 'troops', who were the people most affected by all these changes.

So, you ask, did I get a new job out of all this? No, officially I was still a member of the computer project team, two years after my last involvement with that worthy outfit; and I could still get no decision from anyone about where I was to go next, despite making various suggestions that seemed reasonable enough to me.

I was being made to feel like a problem, and yet I could not see what problem I was to the police service. I had never done it any harm that I knew of and simply wanted to get on with things. Without malice towards the individuals concerned, I reflected on some of the real personnel problems that had arisen in recent years, like the newly promoted superintendent who had shot himself dead in his own station armoury, the superintendent who was jailed for a year for misappropriating police club funds and the superintendent who was found in a compromising situation in a police station with a cleaner. On a scale of personnel problems that these kinds of debacle represented for the decision makers in our organisation, I did not even register.

So there was still nothing for it but to get myself back to my mounds of PACE Act papers. The Act was in force and the people in the divisional stations where the police work had to be done were doing a very good job in handling all the new procedures and documents I had been obliged to send them. Even so, the changes were so many and varied that queries about interpretation and application of the new legislation were bound to arise, and I found it satisfying to act in an advisory/consultancy capacity, within the county of Cumbria and elsewhere.

I was now approaching another 'career management interview' with the chief constable and deputy chief. I did not have to submit myself to this process but nevertheless decided it would be best if I did. As usual, there had been no discussion with anyone beforehand (although at least now I knew my personnel record was accurate because I had got the necessary additions done) and there was to be no counselling or de-briefing afterwards.

The chief opened by asking if I thought I had 'wasted my time on the computer project team'. The answer to that one was obvious because of course I had been prevented right from the outset from exerting any kind of restraining influence – so badly needed, in my view – on my 'young and enthusiastic' colleagues. Seeing no value at all in making that contentious point to the chief, I confined myself to a non-committal answer.

The deputy chief followed up with another point about

the computer system, which was now 'up and running' at all the control centres: 'Divisional commanders tell me the system needs to be constantly fed by the controllers with information while producing nothing of value in return. What are your views on that?'

My true answer to that should have been on the lines of 'Well, you must have agreed to go ahead with the computer system, yet you seemed to take no interest in how it was proceeding. Knowing me as you do, you should know I would have urged commonsense and restraint, with the controllers' workload very much in mind.' While that would have been the honest answer, I simply confined myself to saying I could not answer that or any other criticism of the computer system because I had never worked with it in practice.

The deputy continued with, 'Don't you think there should be some before/after evaluation?'

My true view on that one was, 'Yes, of course there should be but that is for you to decide, not me. If there is such an evaluation (which I am sure there won't be) then I will be pleased to take part in it.' Of course, I did not actually say that in reply to the deputy chief's question but simply agreed that it sounded a good idea.

This was 1986 and criticism of police methods and management was mounting in the media. Even the *Daily Telegraph* (supposedly the policeman's newspaper) was wondering what was happening and calling for a 'wholesale review of the organisation of policing'. And yet complacency was everywhere in the senior levels of the police service. The attitude was 'Why worry? – our index-linked pay keeps coming through. Let's apply for more funds and more staff and resist all demands from outside for a say in what we do with them.' The atmosphere of complacency at the upper echelons was redolent of the drunk falling from the top of the high building and shouting to the horrified onlookers in each floor on the way down – 'OK so far!'

There was so much to do and I was so keen to have a go, but clearly I was still 'out on a limb.' Soon after the 'career management interview' I put in an application for consideration as a candidate for the Bramshill Fellowship Scheme. This would have given me 'a year's research into a subject directly related to current policing problems and thus of value to the police service,' as the Home Office blurb put it, under the supervision of the Police College and of a university. With the police getting a lot of bad press, I chose Public Relations from the list of approved subjects for study and submitted a preliminary report outlining my proposals.

While I considered myself perfectly capable of doing this project, both from a practical and an academic point of view, recent experiences suggested I should not be too optimistic, but I had tried just about everything else. I didn't get it. Apparently the chief thought 'it would not be in the police interest at present.'

So it was back to 'Gizza job.' The months passed and I was being paid over £15,000 a year for using about ten per cent of my ability. Suddenly, getting on for three years after I first started asking 'What next?' and getting nowhere, I got an unsigned bit of paper from some Jobsworth in the field of personnel. It gave me about a week's notice of a transfer to traffic (administration). This must have been about the lowest-status inspector's job in the force, but protest would have got me nowhere so I reported to the traffic department as instructed.

The chief superintendent in charge of the traffic department was a long-standing friend of mine who sympathised with my point of view about the job in his department. Maybe also he did not fancy the idea of one so disgruntled as me on his staff, but in any case he did offer to accompany me on an appeal to the deputy chief constable. I declined the chief superintendent's kind offer with thanks as at that point I could not think how to approach the problem in any way I had not tried already.

The following Saturday morning I was off duty and went into police headquarters to see the deputy chief constable. Getting the all clear from his secretary, I knocked on his office door and went in. He looked up from his desk and said, 'I've only got a minute.'

I replied, 'That's all right, sir, I only need a minute. As you know, I've been without a specific job for two or three years. You have resolved the problem by sending me to Traffic Admin. and I've come to thank you for that.'

The deputy chief constable jumped up from his chair, looking quite startled. He said, 'You'd better sit down.'

I answered, 'No, thank you. You said you only had a minute and I've said all I have to say. Good morning.' He did not look happy. I left.

While I had been dished a real problem with this Traffic Admin. thing, it was some small comfort to know that friends and colleagues in the organisation were obviously not too impressed either. One morning at coffee in the Mess (pique did not cause me to miss the coffee ritual) the detective chief superintendent remarked, 'So they've sent you to Traffic Admin?' He looked thoughtful. Pretending to be philosophical about it, I replied, 'Could be worse.' He said, 'Not much.' He was right. Laconic, we Cumbrians.

Soon afterwards I got a call from the second-in-command of the Traffic Department. A decent, genuine man whom I considered a long-standing friend, he had earlier listened to an outline of my tribulations arising from membership of the computer project team and had hazarded a guess at the cause that was remarkably near the truth.

Big Nev looked uncomfortable. He pulled at his shirt collar and said, 'You're not going to like this. It looks as if you're on the move again. I've got the deputy chief on the 'phone. He wants to know how soon you can get over to complaints and discipline.' Still being fairly light on my feet, I could probably have done the 50 yards in about five seconds. However, I did not want to upset my old friend by making it so obvious how much I wanted to be out of his department. It was a Thursday. For his sake I put on an air of resignation and said, 'Next Monday should do.'

'OK,' said Big Nev, 'I'll tell him next Monday,' and off he went.

I was more than pleased. In all the circumstances I could not have wished for a better move. Among all the other suggestions I had put forward in this long period of limbo that I had endured, I had asked to go to the Complaints and Discipline Department without even getting a comment in reply. Now it seemed 'they' could not get me there fast enough. And I had just gone to all the trouble of thanking the deputy chief constable for sending me to Traffic…

The last few years in the police service had been something of a roller-coaster for me. I had joined the computer project team with some misgivings but took it on in the belief that my eighteen years' police experience and my personal qualities, such as they were, had been taken into account. It had been a shock to discover that the team leader had seen me as some sort of fifth-columnist with a wrecking brief, and his delusional ideas had clearly found fertile ground with at least one influential member of the force hierarchy who did not know him as well as I did.

The computer/communications system that was envisaged when I joined the team was ambitious and complex, and the recommended early stages of planning were being by-passed. To my mind, we were totally disregarding the normal standards of transparency, commonsense and restraint that should characterise any worthwhile police activity, and I had put my concerns clearly in writing. The unaccountably hostile response had been to my detriment as well as, I venture to say, to the detriment of the project because my potential contribution was so devalued.

Further disappointment came with eventual discovery that I had not been rehabilitated by the planning I did for the police response to the miners' strike or, more especially, by all the effort involved in sorting out the implications of the major new Police and Criminal Evidence Act and putting it into practice in Cumbria.

Mind you, I was not entirely blameless in all this because I had left myself answerable to one or two people – ex-cadets to a man, I'm afraid – who really and bluntly were not up to their jobs in any organisation that was in touch with reality. But it was of little consolation to know that I was not alone in that assessment.

My otherwise forgettable few months with the routine paperwork of the headquarters traffic department were pleasantly interrupted early on by a four-week sojourn by the seaside at the Yorkshire resort of Scarborough. I hasten to say it was not a spell of rest and recuperation, however badly that may have been needed in my case, but a very welcome interlude nevertheless.

For these four weeks I was privileged to take part in a marking panel assessing the results of recent police promotion examinations. My colleagues and I who had been assembled for the task from all over the north of England were accommodated for the duration in a rather grand cliff-top hotel that had been the ancestral home of the family of the distinguished actor Charles Laughton.

The oak-panelled ambience of the four-star establishment, quietly out-of-season as it was at the time, was entirely suited to the gravity of our task. The hospitality and the food provided were of a very high standard, and it was here that

I became addicted to a previously unfamiliar delicacy called sticky toffee pudding, which featured on virtually every evening dinner menu and appeared to be a very successful speciality of the management of this hotel.

There was much talk among us panelists of the perhaps inevitable problem of putting on weight during our well fed and not particularly stressful time at the old Laughton establishment on its vantage point overlooking the North Sea at Scarborough. Without seriously suggesting that the effect of our combined appetites had been a decisive factor in what subsequently befell the prominent landmark that had been our shared place of residence for a month, the fate of this fine hotel may be of interest for it is true to say it went downhill rapidly soon after we left.

I had been back at home at Penrith for only a matter of weeks when the national television news featured the shockingly spectacular sight of our erstwhile home for those memorable four weeks in Scarborough falling victim to coastal erosion as it quickly crumbled into the waters of the North Sea some 200 feet below. Irrelevant no doubt, but I could not help looking for some omen in this.

7
COMPLAINTS AND DISCIPLINE

I never did like that title – but I was quite pleased to report to the headquarters department with the ominous-sounding name in December 1986. There were just three of us based there – three police members, that is – plus the lady who kept the files straight and remembered everything that the rest of us forgot about, like court dates and appointments.

The man in charge was a superintendent I had known for many years. Like me, he was a Cumbrian from the west of the county. Indeed, we had attended the same school for a time all those years ago, and both of us had done our national service in the Army at the height of the Cold War in the 1950s, so we had quite a lot in common. A rumbustious sort of man with a keen sense of humour, super Len's personal reputation was centred around his ability to avoid spending a pound if a penny would do, and he was certainly careful with his brass. A pretty handy wheeler-dealer in his spare time, he had an air of affluence about him that was apparent from the cut of his suits and his scruffy old Volvo car with over 100,000 miles on the clock.

Like any self-respecting Cumbrian, Len liked to call a spade a spade and could seem quite blunt at times – abrasive, in fact, to people who had not known him as long as I had. I suppose neither of us was the sort to suffer fools gladly or back down too readily, and our long-standing friendship had been tested just a few weeks earlier in a brief dispute over a matter to do with the PACE Act planning.

He had told me in his own inimitable way to do a new Force Order arising out of sections of the new Act that were concerned with complaints against police. My terms of reference in dealing with this Act were that I should prepare new or amended Force Orders only when there was no headquarters department affected by a new provision of the Act. If there was, then the headquarters department concerned (eg CID, Traffic) would be responsible for preparing the new guidance. This clearly applied also to HQ Complaints and Discipline, and I told him so as forcefully as he had told me to get it done. The brief encounter had taken place over the telephone, and my old friend ended it by shouting 'Well, I'm going to see about this!' and slamming the 'phone down.

At the time I had been attached to the force Planning Department, so I thought I had better mention this brief but heated exchange to the man in charge of that department. I was in his small office a few minutes later, standing casually in front of his desk, when the door burst open and super Len shot in. Catching me unawares and off-balance, he hit me full in the chest and knocked me flying backwards into a chair. This was a full frontal assault before a witness, far more acceptable than the back-stabbing – yes, I can't find any other way of describing it – that I had experienced in my previous assignment not all that long before. I jumped to my feet and squared up to my assailant, until the altercation was ended by intervention from the gentleman whose office and hospitality we were abusing, with the impassioned plea, 'Oh, hell, lads, let's cool it!' Good sense prevailed and Len reluctantly accepted that his Force Order was outside my terms of reference.

Not one to bear a grudge, super Len welcomed me wholeheartedly to his little domain just a few weeks later. Indeed, he might well have had a say in getting me there. Mind you, he was not so daft. Unlike one or two lesser souls who clearly had been seeking to dent my self-esteem and reputation in recent times, Len had the sense to see that my talents, such as they were, might as well be used, and used in his department at that.

It seemed his confidence in me was not misplaced – over the first couple of weeks I took on about half a dozen complaint files that were awaiting attention and met the people concerned, and the allegation in each case was either withdrawn or not pursued by the complainant with a written statement in confirmation. Not always fulsome in his praise, my new leader was moved to exclaim, 'By Jove, you're a dab hand (an 'expert', in the Cumbrian vernacular) at this!' Praise indeed.

I should say at this point that the procedure was that every complaint by a member of the public against a police officer, once officially registered at police headquarters, had to be thoroughly investigated in accordance with the prescribed rules, if necessary culminating in court proceedings or a disciplinary hearing before the chief constable. In practice, however, what usually represented success in the investigator's art was the result 'complaint withdrawn' or – almost as good – 'not pursued'.

This was not so much a matter of deviousness as of plain commonsense founded on experience. A conviction under the criminal law required evidence of guilt beyond reasonable doubt, and the standard of proof in police disciplinary proceedings was just the same. In dealing with public complaints against police you soon found that the chances of achieving that sort of evidence were just about nil in the vast majority of cases.

Most complaints against police were in the area of abuse of authority, in the sense that a policeman had been uncivil while reporting an offender for summons or was supposed to have assaulted or roughly handled someone who was being arrested. Obviously in such a case the complainant had an axe to grind, and that was not the ideal basis for starting an inquiry possibly leading to proceedings. Very often the evidence was simply not there: the complainant was there at the time so he knew what happened, or thought he knew, but there was no-one else to support his story so it could only be weighed against a denial of misconduct by the police officer. Many complainants had been drinking and others had already lumbered themselves with a list of criminal convictions.

Policemen were usually very worried about getting complaints against them and naturally did not readily admit to wrongdoing in these circumstances. They obviously had to know a bit about evidence so they were not going to give too much away against themselves. They naturally 'closed ranks' when one of their number was in trouble, and even members of the public who were potential witnesses in complaint cases were not always happy about providing evidence against the police. Then again, many complainants did not really want to be involved in all the rigmarole of evidence-gathering and formal proceedings, preferring instead to tell their problem to someone in authority who was prepared to listen, in the belief that he would sort it out for them in his own way and that would be the end of the matter.

In criminal allegations against police officers the Director of Public Prosecutions had to decide on the question of proceedings, and for sound practical reasons he would only give the go-ahead if he thought there was more than a 50% chance of conviction. Despite supposedly declining public esteem for the police, juries generally were not too keen to convict policemen.

So there were all sorts of reasons why the statistics for complaints against the police usually showed a substantiated rate of about 1%. This did not mean that 99% were false or that there had been a massive police cover-up. It just indicated that there had not been the evidence to prove that the alleged wrongs happened – or did not happen, for that matter – even if all the complainants wanted things to go that far.

With this sort of knowledge of practicalities, any sensible police officer dealing with a complaint would want to be a conciliator before he was obliged to be an investigator. There was not much point in rushing straight out to every complaint with a good stock of statement forms to greet the complainant with something like: 'Good morning, sir, my name's Inspector Bloggs and I'm here to take your detailed statement with a view to a full investigation into your complaint and possible criminal or discipline proceedings.'

Full complaint inquiries could take months to finalise, and 'working to rule' like that would have soon bogged the whole system down. Then again, having regard to all the factors in the way of a positive outcome, it would often be simply unfair to the complainant to set him off on an investigation that had no prospect of 'convicting' the alleged wrong-doer. As with many policing problems, it was usually far better to take it slowly in the expectation that – with a little bit of help from you – the thing would eventually sort itself out, or at least not get any worse than it was already.

If there was a question of preserving evidence, then you may have had to take some immediate action. In most cases, though, on getting a complaint to deal with, the best thing to do at first was just to leave it for a week or so. You could find out what was on record about the complainant, particularly whether he had any criminal convictions or had made complaints against police before. If his complaint arose out of the circumstances of his arrest, there would be a detailed record of events at the police station concerned called a custody record, and getting hold of a copy of that was always useful. And what about the police officer(s) concerned, particularly age and length of service? Any record of previous complaints against them? Stick all the papers in a folder and put them to one side for now. Let things start to go off the boil. If proceedings had been started against the complainant, await the outcome and make every effort to be there when the case came to court.

When you thought you were getting towards the right time to see the complainant you could try and contact them by telephone. Most people, even the most villainous (or maybe especially the most villainous) were on the 'phone. Treat any telephone conversation as a vital first step in dealing with the complainant. Listen to him if he wanted to talk about his problem and don't get off on the wrong foot. You had to remember that he would be forming impressions of you just as you were assessing him. You had to achieve some kind of rapport with him if you were going to deal with the matter in the best way for all concerned.

Obviously you had not to put the complainant to any inconvenience. He already had a grievance against the police, real or imaginary, and you could not afford to make it any worse. You had to be prepared to go to his home rather than meeting at a police station.

When you went to the house you didn't go in police uniform and you didn't park a marked police vehicle outside. You didn't want to cause any embarrassment with the neighbours, did you? If possible, it was best to go on your own. This showed confidence and avoided any appearance that you were trying to intimidate the complainant by outnumbering him.

It was vital to have plenty of time to get there and be punctual, so that you did not have to start with an apology for lateness. Not all complainants against police were entirely reliable, but there was no need to bother yourself if he or she did not turn up at the agreed time. If they were not there, you could leave and start the process again when you were ready. This time they might feel the need to apologise to you for their absence the first time, and that could well be a point to you right at the outset.

When you had got your meeting arranged, it was best not to be over-formal in your approach. Ideally, leave your briefcase behind (although I remember being in at least one house where I was glad to have my heavy leather bag handy as a defensive weapon). You could always refresh your memory on the contents of the complaint file just before going into the house. For obvious reasons, you certainly had to be able to discuss the problem without having to refer to a pile of papers. It had got to look as if it was as big an issue to you as it was to the complainant, so you knew all about it, didn't you?

Courtesy had to be the watch-word right from the start. Some people lived in appalling squalor but you had not even to blink at that, although I have seen houses where you had to be careful where you put your feet, let alone your behind. You had to try and gain the complainant's confidence. Tell him or her something about yourself and let them talk about their situation – family, job, interests – anything to relax the inevitable tension.

Gradually of course you got round to the real purpose of your visit. You asked him – or her, but not many complainants were ladies – to explain the problem from the start, and you did not interrupt unnecessarily. At the same time you had to look interested and concerned. You had come to help sort out the problem, so be human about it. Above all, never argue with the complainant. Falling out would get you nowhere. You had to bear in mind that they were no doubt there when the incident happened (unlike you), so knew what happened – whether or not they were telling you the truth about it – and they could be absolutely right. Agree with the complainant where you could.

Furthermore, a complaint investigator never had to be on

the defensive. In particular, the investigator had not to jump to the defence of the police force. Things do go wrong at times and, let's face it, this could be one occasion where they really have. Even if you could not see anything wrong, you had to be wary about saying that. Better to let him or her tell you why it was wrong.

In general, it was best to do far more listening than talking. Let the person tell you exactly why they did not like the police force or individuals in it. Let them get it all off their chest. At the same time look out for any natural breaks to ease the tension and accept any offers of hospitality in the way of a cup of tea or whatever – although facing up to that in some houses could be way beyond the call of duty, I can tell you.

Finally, you had to assess what the person wanted as an outcome from their complaint. If they really seemed to want prosecution or formal discipline proceedings, what was the strength of the evidence? Explain the degree of proof required and were they prepared to go to court or police headquarters to give evidence? If they had any witnesses, would they be ready to do the same? If the complainant was looking for some sort of compensation, that was a matter for his solicitor. Ideally, let a course emerge, if possible, without pressuring the complainant or presenting them with a set of options. If you had gained their confidence, they might want you to deal with it yourself, although you had not to tell them what you were going to do about it. That was a matter for you, but you had to be prepared to keep faith with the complainant, and you had not to make bargains with them or promise action that was beyond your legal powers.

Whatever course was decided upon, as the investigator you were going to have to get a written statement but the time had to be right. You had not to be too quick to produce a statement form, and you might not get anything at all in writing at a first meeting. You had to be sure you did not stay too long – best to set a time limit of, say, an hour or so. If you had not got a statement signed by then, be prepared to leave and see them again later. Another week or so would not matter, and things may look rather different by then. It may take two or three calls for the right time to emerge to produce a statement form. After all, what you are after in most cases is complaint withdrawn or at least not pursued; and an hour or two of patience at this stage might just avoid umpteen hours doing a full investigation that ends up not substantiated and makes nobody any happier.

It was the late 1980s and we had a new Police and Criminal Evidence Act that was all about police accountability and had no less than 23 sections on the subject of complaints against the police. How did the police force of the day swing into action to deal with a complaint from the public? Let me give a few examples.

As mentioned, I had some early successes in getting complaints withdrawn or not pursued. Most were dealt with like that but inevitably some would not be quite so easily resolved.

We had a complaint from two ladies living in the far south of the county. They were a middle-aged woman and her 20-year-old daughter who were alleging gross incivility by a young constable, claiming in fact that he had sworn at them in no uncertain terms. The allegation had been recorded in the complaints register and the usual letter of acknowledgement had gone off to say that a senior police officer would get in touch in the near future.

The appropriate checks indicated that the two ladies did not have any convictions recorded against them and did not appear to have made any previous complaints against police. Being quite new to the department, I did not know the constable concerned, but a check of the records revealed that he was 23 years of age with just over two years' service but had no less than twelve complaints from the public against him in the last eighteen months. This 'score' was way beyond anything in my experience. The allegations were all in the area of abuse of authority (i.e. incivility or minor assaults) and all had ended up either withdrawn or not pursued. Without any disrespect to the young man concerned, who for all I knew might have been the victim of a concerted campaign of vilification, I am afraid I have to reveal that his name was PC Thicke. Like me, he had an 'e' on the end of an otherwise undistinguished monosyllabic surname, and I was to learn subsequently that a further refinement was that the final 'e' was used to effect a pronunciation that rhymed with 'like'.

I left things a week or so and then contacted the elder of the two complainants by telephone. Naturally it always gave you a bit of an advantage, when dealing with a complaint from a member of the public, to say you were speaking from police headquarters rather than from the local station. Anyway, the call was a success in the sense that some initial rapport was indicated, and arrangements were made to see the complainant and her daughter at their home address the following week. For the complainant, things were moving but the problem might just have simmered down a bit by the time we met, around two weeks after the event.

In the meantime, something happened that revealed our young constable in a very enterprising light. At the time of the alleged encounter with the two ladies he had been accompanied by a special constable. Anticipating a complaint by the ladies, he had somehow managed to persuade a young female colleague to take a written statement from the special constable in which the point was made that he, PC Thicke, had conducted himself with restraint in the face of hostility. This proved to be a master stroke.

Eventually we met the two ladies. Far be it from me to

want to appear anything less than gallant, but I would not have thought them so sensitive as to be devastated by hearing a bit of flowery language, and the situation was complicated to some extent by the fact they both knew the young constable personally. Indeed, it seemed possible that the young man might have attempted some romantic liaison with the daughter in the past.

Taking the personal aspects with the special constable's statement, I thought the chances of achieving a substantiated complaint here were just about nil. We went through the usual rigmarole of courtesy to the two complainants, admiring their home with its sea views, drinking copious amounts of tea, stroking the cat and so on, but all to no avail. The ladies had a deep-seated grievance against our young constable, so in the end we just had to get on with it and record their detailed statements forming the basis of a full disciplinary investigation.

There were no truly independent witnesses to what had happened between the constable and the two complainants. Whether we liked it or not, we had the special constable's statement which was more favourable to the accused constable than to the ladies. When we saw this man we were not at all happy with his account of events as set out in this unwanted statement but naturally, having signed it, he could not now go back on what he had said in it.

The young policewoman who had recorded the special constable's statement was quite upset about it when we saw her, but it was clearly all down to her inexperience and she had become involved in the affair in all innocence.

Eventually, the superintendent and I fixed a time for a formal interview with the constable who was at the centre of this little storm. We did not tell him we were coming to see him in case he went sick or did something else to avoid us. By now I had discovered that my leader had had previous dealings with the constable and indeed had dealt with several of the earlier complaints against him that had been withdrawn or not pursued. I had no idea what efforts had been made to bring the remarkable run of complaints to an end, but clearly in this case he was out to 'have' this young man and no messing this time.

It was 9.30am on a fine summer's day when we got the anonymous grey complaints department car out of the garage at police HQ and set off south on the one and a half hour drive to the far outpost of the county. It was a familiar journey that took us along the southern fringe of the Lake District, and spirits were high despite the unhappy nature of our primary mission that day.

Soon after half way to our destination we were in need of refuelling (us, not the car), so we pulled in on the usual lay-by on the A590 at Derek's Snax. I did say my friend the superintendent was careful with his brass, and at 20p per mug this was by far the cheapest tea we could find in the area. Of course, you did not have to reflect too much on how the proprietor of the said mobile enterprise by the roadside did his washing up. Anyway, we got our steaming mugs of tea and stood in the sunshine on the lay-by among the lorry drivers. I had noticed that Derek had called me 'Sir' as he served us while he had addressed super Len as 'mate', but that was probably because my well dressed friend had discarded his jacket to reveal his braces.

Suitably refreshed, we pressed on. We knew our 'suspect' was due to start duty at 2pm, and at that time, after dealing with one or two lesser commitments, we were firmly ensconced in the local chief superintendent's office which was not in use that day. It was a well-rehearsed routine. As usual, I would sit behind the desk with a good supply of 'contemporaneous record of interview' forms while my colleague sat off to one side where he was well-placed to fire the questions. Everything that was said by the interviewer and the interviewee had to be recorded at the time so the whole thing had to be done at dictation speed. This could naturally make it all seem a bit artificial but it could still be quite hard going for the scribbler, which in this case was going to be me.

A few minutes later our young constable was standing in the corridor outside the office. Still clearly determined to 'have' him this time, my fiery friend said by way of final briefing to me, 'Right, I want every single word recorded of this interview with this bloody man, everything!'

I nodded and went out to fetch the young constable. He was understandably very nervous. I noticed he had a marked facial twitch which I later learned was a long-standing problem for him but was particularly troublesome when he was under pressure. He was under a lot of pressure now.

The young man took the hot seat opposite me. His face seemed to be twitching uncontrollably and I felt a bit concerned about him. Obviously he was very nervous about having to face two middle-aged men in grey suits from the dreaded Complaints Department, but I was soon to discover that he was probably more in control of himself than was apparent at first sight.

I had my pen poised and super Len got straight down to business, barking at the young constable: 'PC Thicke, why are you twitching?' I was slightly taken aback by this, but my job was to do the recording so down the question went on paper, word perfect.

Having stopped writing, I looked at the constable to indicate I was ready for his reply. Seemingly struggling to compose himself, he said, 'Because I am nervous of you'. The reply was duly recorded, and then I looked back at my colleague.

Super Len snapped, 'Why are you nervous of me?' Blasé as I was, I was startled by the response which, being rather longer than the few brief exchanges up to then, had to be taken down in three parts, as dictated to me by the young constable: 'Because the last time – you interviewed me – you assaulted me.'

Pause for me to dot the end of the sentence, then it was my colleague's turn: 'How did I assault you?'

'You kicked me – under the table.'

Super Len's composure was declining as our young hero's seemed to be increasing: 'I have never assaulted anyone in my life,' he asserted.

With a start like this, there was clearly no prospect of a worthwhile interview about the allegations against the constable that we were supposed to be investigating. The interview was abandoned and the whole thing was handed over to a new investigating officer with me as his assistant. In a virtuoso performance belying his unfortunate name, the young constable was winning hands down. You had to admire him.

I put the new man in the picture, and eventually we set off south to start the formal interview all over again. It turned out to be a long one – my written record was twelve pages – but our young hero handled it quite well, although I thought he was perhaps a bit too clever at one point. When asked why he had taken it upon himself to ask the young policewoman to take the special constable's statement, he said it was because of his ignorance of the discipline procedure!

At the end of the formal interview, I abandoned my largely passive role of recorder and told the constable in no uncertain terms that his career in the complaints field now had to be at an end. It may have been a touch brutal but it did seem to me to be long overdue. Anyway, I was not aware of any further complaints against this young man.

We got the report done and the whole thing went off to the independent Police Complaints Authority for their decision on the question of formal discipline proceedings. The Police Complaints Authority were mired up with reports of this sort, and as usual their reply took about six weeks to arrive. We had had to recommend that discipline proceedings were not justified because of the conflicting evidence, and the Police Complaints Authority agreed.

Some four months after the inquiry began the Police Complaints Authority wrote to the complainants to inform them of their decision in the matter. This produced a very hostile reaction from the elder of the two ladies, who wrote to us to say she thought it was scandalous that a policeman should be able to 'get away with' such conduct. Of course, it was all a question of weight of evidence, but she could hardly be expected to understand such technicalities, however carefully and reasonably the Police Complaints Authority explained the situation to her. As far as she was concerned she had been sworn at, and that was that.

As so often in these cases, I wished the aggrieved parties had not pursued the complaint in the first place and left us to deal with it in our own inimitable way. It would not have undone anything that had happened but it would have been quicker than the official way. And, more importantly, the two ladies might have been happier because they could have drawn their own conclusions about what the police force (as personified by two courteous men who had come all the way from police headquarters to see them) had done to deal with a young man who had so offended them, rather than getting a letter to say nothing was being done about it as far as they could see.

Without wanting to labour the point, we had our own way of making a lasting impression on young policemen who were clearly having trouble controlling a tendency to abuse their authority. In essence it involved giving them a sharp taste of their own medicine by slightly abusing our own authority over them. I thought I adopted the procedure very sparingly where there was a clear pattern from previous incidents, and it was intended to be strictly constructive, never damaging. The point was that the full disciplinary investigation process usually took far too long to be in anyone's interests.

Very occasionally, however, you came across a complaint against police where you felt from the outset that it would be best for those concerned to be put through the full inquiry process. One such incident in particular comes to mind and has to do with the circumstances of an arrest for alleged breach of the peace. I suppose its gravity or otherwise depends on one's view of the seriousness of depriving someone of their liberty, even for a short period of time. This particular occurrence was also interesting to me in the sense that it brought into quite sharp focus the old sort of 'minimum action' way of dealing with minor street incidents as opposed to the later kind of 'no messing – lock 'em up' police approach perhaps generated by ready availability of back-up vehicles and radios.

It was the end of a summer carnival day in a small Cumbrian town and the market place was full of people emerging from public houses. There was a larger police presence in the town centre than usual because of a bit of trouble at the previous year's event. A locally based foot patrol constable – a man of the old school of policing and a right PC Plod if ever there was one, but no disrespect to him for that – was standing discreetly in a darkened shop doorway when he noticed two young men struggling with each other some little distance away. At his usual measured pace he went over to them and parted them with a suitable warning.

The problem was effectively over, but the girlfriend of one of the participants was still remonstrating with her boyfriend over his part in the affair a few seconds later when our two over-zealous uniformed heroes screeched to a stop in their large blue van. I should say at this point that the nineteen year old girl, like her companions, was wearing a black leather jacket and jeans. Suddenly, by her subsequent account, she was held from behind in a 'vice-like grip' around her neck and virtually flung into the back of the police van, which then drove round to the police station a few hundred yards away.

When our arresting officer took his prize into the lit interior of the police station someone was heard to exclaim, 'Hey, that's a girl!' Clearly it was only then it was realised that the 'drunk and disorderly' prisoner was female, and she was released without charge soon afterwards. She returned to the police station the next day to lodge a complaint of unjustified arrest and rough handling.

When I saw the girl a week or so later, I found her to be a well-built young woman who could not possibly have been mistaken for male by anyone who heard her voice or looked at her from the front for more than about a millisecond. I had no reason to doubt her account of events, which in any case was supported by others present at the time – including the old-style bobby.

Personally, I thought it was a sordid little incident that brought no credit at all on the police and was even less impressed when I read the constable's duty report justifying his arrest. The usual weeks and months elapsed while efforts were made to find and get statements from all possible witnesses, and eventually we were in a position to interview the two young men from the police van.

No doubt they would not quickly forget their interviews with us, the not always popular headquarters complaint investigators, and it was to be hoped that they would have learned something from the whole sorry problem they brought about. The inquiry ended about six months after it

THE POLICE AND ME

began, with 'suitable disciplinary action' being taken. It was a pity, though, that the job did not have any official means of sending back to square one people who did not seem to have grasped some of the rudiments of policing, like the fact that in real life we did not have anything to learn from *Starsky and Hutch*.

While I am being critical, I might as well relate the circumstances of another arrest that led to an even more agonised complaint against a member of our organisation. In this case, I think it is fair to say I was less than impressed with what was done in the name of policing but could not make any kind of issue out of it because the complainant was found guilty in court of a number of offences arising out of his encounter with the policeman concerned.

It was about 4pm and a car with a disabled driver badge in the window was parked on double-yellow lines in a busy street at the entrance to a city shopping centre. The driver was a middle-aged man with an apparent history of heart trouble. As he was leaving the car with his wife and daughter to go into a nearby shop, he was approached by a policeman who asked him to remove the vehicle on the grounds that it was causing an obstruction of the roadway. He did not comply at that point but said he was going into the shop. Things went rapidly downhill from there.

When the driver got back to his car, he found the policeman had made out a fixed penalty notice (parking ticket) which he was placing under the wiper blade in the approved fashion. The car driver became enraged, tearing the parking ticket off the windscreen and throwing it on the ground, before getting in the vehicle with his family and driving the short distance to the police station to complain about the attitude of the policeman.

A few minutes later the man was in the front entrance of the police station with his wife and daughter. Unfortunately, very unfortunately, the uniformed subject of his grievance then arrived at the same place, and another scene developed in which the man was arrested and dragged off inside the building leaving the two women having hysterics in the hallway.

The car driver was reported for summons for no less than four offences: unnecessary obstruction of the highway, depositing litter (the parking ticket), breach of the peace at the scene and a further breach of the peace at the police station. A complaint was recorded from him about the manner of the reporting policeman and this had to await the outcome of the court proceedings.

The matter took five months to come before the magistrates, and the car driver/complainant pleaded not guilty to all four charges. He conducted his own defence (which is not always a wise thing to do) and was found guilty on all counts, being fined a total of £75 and ordered to pay £90 costs. The hearing had been a long drawn-out affair and the defendant had not exactly charmed the magistrates, but I was surprised at the result. I say that because it was my own view, for what it was worth, that there was basically just one offence here – the unnecessary obstruction with the vehicle – and the other issues had arisen out of a clash of personalities.

In the usual way of these things, I listened to the court proceedings and introduced myself to the complainant afterwards. Not surprisingly, it was not the best time to talk to him about his grievance against the policeman so I arranged to see him later at his home.

We met a few days later for a discussion that took a lot longer than the hour or so I usually set myself for these things. The trouble was, he was a particularly dogmatic sort of gent who had great difficulty accepting that his misfortunes were any fault of his, and letting him 'get it all off his chest' was a considerable trial of patience for me. Dogs were patted, cat stroked, tea drunk and wife engaged in conversation as far as possible in the tirade from him, but it was nearly three hours before I was able to produce a statement form from my pocket and start writing. In short, he signed a statement acknowledging his convictions for the various offences and withdrawing his complaint against the policeman.

He seemed particularly impressed among all the badinage, perhaps even distracted, by my suggestion that it could all have been a case of *de minimis non curat lex*. At his request I wrote the phrase down on a piece of paper for him as he signed the statement. Of course, he had not the foggiest idea what it meant but he did put the piece of paper carefully to one side. (For anyone without Latin it is a legal principle that means 'the law is not concerned with trifles', e.g. driving at 31mph in a 30mph area, stealing a penny or whatever, where technically an offence has been committed but is not worth pursuing).

As I took my leave at last, my new-found friend said he was not going to pay the fines and costs, but that was no concern of mine. A statement withdrawing the complaint was all I wanted here, and I had that in my pocket. Whatever misgivings I had about the policeman concerned, I might as well keep them to myself because of the convictions against the complainant. It was not quite the end of the whole affair, though.

A week or two later I was off duty in a local hostelry when I was approached by a solicitor whom I knew quite well. He assumed an aggrieved air and demanded to know what I thought I was doing quoting the *de minimis* rule to his client!

I was to learn subsequently that the 'client' appealed against the four convictions against him, but the Crown Court dismissed all the matters of appeal except the litter offence, which was allowed, and he was ordered to pay another £140 costs. The fines and costs imposed at the two hearings remained unpaid, and this middle-aged gentleman was brought back to court just over a year after the original incident with his car and sent to prison for fourteen days.

After that final court hearing the officially-disabled hero of this little epic was held in the police cells for a matter of hours to await escort to prison. As always in these cases, a custody record was made out and all the property in his possession at the time was listed. When I saw the property list, I could not help a wry smile to myself at the contrast between this middle-aged man's belongings and those of the average young male taken into police custody for theft, violence, breach of the peace or whatever. Instead of the usual 'cigarettes, matches and 53 pence in coins' kind of thing, here we had 'walking-stick, spectacles and three bottles of pills'. Still, justice obviously was taking its course.

Nothing more was heard of this issue for another nine months, when the man wrote us an anguished letter about his disgust at going to prison and his hatred for the policeman concerned. Nothing could be done in any official sense but it was only human to call and see him. When I met him a week or two later, I found him even angrier than he was before, because of his experiences at the appeal court and in prison.

There was no point in staying with him very long, but at least he smiled slightly at one thing that happened in the prison where he did his fourteen days.

After going through the usual reception process on arrival, he was escorted to a cell and the door clanged shut behind him. It was a terrible shock to a middle-aged man who had not been in trouble before. He sat down on the bunk bed, totally dejected. He noticed there was a young man lying on the bunk opposite. Eventually the young man said, 'Fancy a fag, pop?' Having had his cigarettes taken off him at reception, our hero said he would indeed like a smoke.

Warming noticeably to his subject, my raconteur went on, 'The young bloke got off the bed and dropped his trousers. I thought, "Oh, my God, after all this I'm locked up with one of them." Anyway, it turned out the lad had an artificial leg. He took the leg off, tipped it up and out dropped fags, matches, drugs, all sorts of stuff!'

Soon after this I managed to take my leave. It was now nearly two years since my talkative friend had parked his car in the wrong place in front of the wrong policeman. He was no nearer coming to terms with it but there was nothing the police could do to help him.

Talking of prison, complaints investigation often involved visiting people behind bars. Nothing much else to do while you are locked up, so why not write letters of complaint about the people who put you there? Of course, the fact that an individual was in prison did not deprive him of his right to make a complaint against police. It would be recorded just the same as any other, but I always thought in these cases you needed to be especially careful not to finish up having to do a full inquiry. It would probably be a waste of time anyway, and you had to be very conscious of the likely feelings of the policemen complained against.

You needed to leave the prison with a signed statement of complaint withdrawn. How you achieved that result depended to some extent on the individual you were dealing with, but in essence you had to make a good show of being fair with him. After all, you were not one of those nasty policemen, bent, corrupt, violent, perjurious or whatever, who put him there; you were a decent sort who had come all this way specially to listen to his problem and maybe make life a bit harder for the people he hated. The good 'investigator' in these circumstances would do his best to befriend the complainant: it was only for an hour or so, and the prisoner was doing time anyway, whatever happened to his complaint.

A visit to Durham Prison comes to mind. I was with super Len and we were going to see a man from the London area who was doing six years for supplying drugs in our part of the world. We had often done this sort of thing before and thought we were fairly good at it: plenty of listening, agreeing, no arguing and, as the crucial stage of the interview was reached, one doing the talking and one doing the writing. With a bit of luck, our man would have his short statement written out for him and signed without hardly noticing what had happened.

Durham was a fairly typical Victorian establishment of the sort that would be familiar to followers of the television series *Porridge*. Some of these places could smell a bit but this one was not too bad. We identified ourselves at the reception desk and were let in to go upstairs and sit in one of the glass-walled interview rooms to await the production of our complainant.

After a few minutes our man was shown in and we were left alone with him. He was not at all happy about doing six years for an offence for which other people in this place were doing only half that time, as he had discovered. Presumably that was the basis of his grievance but, being unable to do anything about that, I suppose he thought he might as well try and vent some of his anger on the policemen involved.

However, having said his piece, he turned out to be an affable sort of man with whom we struck up a reasonable relationship. He would not pursue his complaint against police but he did want us to enlighten him, if we could, on another aspect of the case that had been troubling him. That was the 'bargain' we agreed upon, and we said we would enquire and let him know the answer to the problem the next time we were back in Durham.

The vital thing now was to get a statement signed while the mood was right. While my colleague kept up the chat, I produced a statement form and started to write. I filled in the standard details at the top of the form – Name: John Wilson; Age: 40; Address: HM Prison Durham. For occupation, where prisoners were concerned, usually I did not bother to ask but simply wrote unemployed. This man, however, had a sense of humour, so I asked him solemnly, 'Occupation, John?' He replied, 'Burglar,' and added, 'Well, let's face it, that's all I've done all my life.' I duly recorded the occupation given. Actually, with his personal qualities, I would have thought he might have done better as a con-man but it was not up to me to offer career advice.

Anyway, our man signed the statement of withdrawal without offering to read it, and we left him to the rest of his sentence.

Back in Durham on other business a few weeks later, we went to see our complainant John Wilson and tell him the result of the little inquiry we had done for him in the meantime. He was very pleased to see us, quite moved in fact, and remarked in his strong southern accent, 'I never thought I'd see you two blokes again.' We assured him we always kept faith with people, and I thought he would have believed that.

As we were leaving, he told us he was hoping to be transferred to another prison farther south. Most of his family had disowned him because of his criminal activities but he thought he might have a better chance of getting a visit from them if he was a bit nearer home. We wished him well.

A matter of months later I was with a colleague in a new high-security prison near York. We were seeing a man who was doing a long stretch for armed robbery. As might be expected, charm was not his strong point, and it was not at all easy to strike up any kind of positive relationship with him. Despite the hostility, however, we eventually managed to get the 'business' done with a suitable written statement withdrawing his complaint against police and were about to take our leave when this character's manner suddenly changed and he became quite human. He looked at me and asked, 'Are you Mr Sharpe?'

Always wanting to be nice to prisoners making complaints against police but at the same time preferring to remain anonymous, I replied warily, 'Ye-es'.

He went on, 'John Wilson. Was in Durham. He's on the same landing as me. Asked me to give you his regards.' Now it was my turn to be quite moved. It really was rather touching. Maybe there is a human side to all of us after all – complainants, convicted criminals, policemen, everybody.

Some complaints against police could be quite funny – in all senses of the word. Having just philosophised about the possibility of humanity in all of us, I nearly said I never met any complainant against police, however hostile at first, with whom I could not eventually achieve some kind of rapport. There was one exception, and it was not the fault of either of us.

We had a complaint from social workers to the effect that a 40 year old man in their care had been assaulted by two policemen. The individual concerned was severely mentally handicapped and had been in residential care since childhood. On the day in question he had been travelling on his own, by train, from one social services establishment to another and had just got off the train when the assault was supposed to have happened.

I was a bit sceptical but, on the face of it, it was a serious allegation and I got on with it straight away. The 'let it cool off' approach was out in this case, obviously.

The social workers were adamant that they had a reliable story but they could add nothing to it. I saw the alleged assault victim but his condition was such that there was no question of communicating with him by any means known to me. In fact he could not communicate with anyone except by means of a very basic sign language which I had never even heard of.

So it was a bit of a problem, and there were more complications to come. It emerged that the first person to hear about the issue was the complainant's elderly father, some days after the event. When I went to see him, I had the greatest difficulty communicating with him also. He was apparently Latvian by birth, with only a limited command of English, and of a very nervous disposition complicated by heart trouble. In fact, it was only with a lot of assistance from his English wife that I was able to get any sort of story from him about what was supposed to have happened to his son. It seemed the wife had passed on the details to the social workers who lodged the complaint with us .

Apparently the elderly gentleman had had some terrible wartime experiences in his native country, and I got the impression that he was frightened of me as a police officer, even though of course I was not in uniform. Regrettably in fact he became tearful, as also in turn did his lady wife and the small baby she had on her knee.

It was all terribly sad but it did make me even more anxious to discover what had happened to their son, or at least do what I could to reassure them that he had not been subjected to violence by the police.

There was nothing in any police record of any involvement with this disabled man. Pausing to reflect on the situation, it occurred to me that what we had here was a fourth-hand complaint starting with a man without effective means of communication trying to tell his story to another man with very poor English before it got anywhere near us. Still, the thing would not go away so I just had to get on with it.

I doubt whether I did get to the bottom of things and sort it all out conclusively, but I was as sure as I could be that there had been no assault by police or indeed any involvement by police at all. To cut a long story short, what seemed to have happened was that when this very handicapped man got off the train there was no one there to meet him so he wandered out of the station and got on a bus. This was travelling in the opposite direction to where he should have been going. He got very agitated and two uniformed bus men tried to make sense of him before taking him back to their depot where office staff eventually managed to contact the people at his intended destination. I could never be sure but I did not think anyone had assaulted this unfortunate individual. Anyway, the social workers were happy to withdraw their complaint against police so I suppose that represented some sort of success.

Only a couple of miles from the institution where the complainant in the last case lived, another incident happened that was to lead to a complaint that a vehicle had been damaged by police. Though totally unrelated, it was round about the same time as the last one also. Maybe it was a phase of the Moon or something .

Two well known members of the local light-fingered fraternity had been seen acting suspiciously, as they say, and made off in a car, closely followed by a police vehicle. A high-speed chase ensued over narrow country roads during which the policemen several times saw articles being thrown from the suspect vehicle. No doubt spurred on by the pursuing blue roof light, the villains' car reached some prodigious speeds before making a sharp left turn into a tarmac driveway which terminated at a vicarage, and the chase ended there.

It was midnight, and apparently the resident vicar had just retired to bed when his darkened room was bathed in an ethereal blue light which caused him momentarily to think it was the second coming! Certainly it was an unusual occurrence in this rural part of the world and the reverend gentleman was agog with it when I saw him a few days later.

The complaint was that one of the policemen had used his truncheon to smash one of the suspects' car windows when the occupants did not get out quickly enough. We also got a claim for £50 compensation for the damage. The two worthies in the car were sentenced to imprisonment for various offences and we eventually 'sorted out' the complaint and the claim.

Coming back down to earth, probably one of the strangest complaints I ever dealt with came from a rather odd young man living near a city centre. What he said was that a police vehicle had been driven dangerously and he had been assaulted by one of the occupants.

It was around 2am and all the drinking clubs were turning out in an area of kebab shops and such like establishments where people were inclined to congregate and trouble was common. It was a fine night and our hero was standing idly watching what was going on. He was dressed in full evening wear including bow-tie and white shirt, having just attended a 'business dinner' – so he said, although in his case I could not imagine what sort of business it could have been. Disorder was breaking out all over the place, and some of the worst offenders were being arrested and bundled into the back of a large police van. Several policemen were at the scene, including an inspector.

The 'businessman'/complainant in all his finery also got himself arrested – not at the scene of the disorder but a few minutes later at the city police station, and accordingly his complaints against police had to be deferred pending the outcome of the proceedings against him.

In the usual way of these things, I attended the court hearing a few weeks later and made notes as the story of the night's events unfolded in evidence before the magistrates.

The eccentric complainant was charged with breach of the peace at the police station and assaulting a policeman. He pleaded not guilty to both charges and the hearing took up the best part of a day in court, mainly because about six policemen had to give evidence for the prosecution but also because of the defendant's flights of fantasy in the witness box. While much of what this young man said in his own defence sounded like arrant nonsense, it was on oath and he appeared to believe it, even if nobody else was likely to believe it.

Our man in the dinner suit had stood watching a number of fighting youths being arrested and shoved into the police van. Two or three policemen, including the inspector, got in the back of the van with the prisoners and the double doors at the rear were slammed shut on the commotion inside. The vehicle then moved off, and as it did so this individual in his dinner suit jumped on the back step. What he intended to do was anybody's guess, but as the vehicle accelerated away he left it too late to jump off, and so he was carried through the city centre hanging onto the door handles in best *Keystone Cops* fashion. The streets were busy at the time and no doubt it was quite a spectacle.

The driver of the police van was unaware of his extra passenger. All he wanted to do was to get to the police station as quickly as possible so he did not hang about. Despite the trouble they were having controlling the prisoners, the policemen in the passenger compartment of the vehicle were aware of the person on the back step. All they could see, though, through the small windows in the rear doors was part of a black suit and white shirt. In fact, they thought it was one of their own colleagues, and the inspector said in evidence that he had intended to reprimand this 'officer' for his highly irregular behaviour when they got to the police station.

As soon as the van stopped in the rear yard of the city police station, the smartly-dressed man on the back-step wrenched open the doors of the vehicle and attacked one of the uniformed policemen inside. However, he was eventually overpowered and dragged under arrest into the cells, in a scene which one experienced policeman said in evidence was the 'worst violence he had ever seen in a police station'. (Funnily enough, I thought I had heard this man say that before in the witness box, but anyway it sounded quite convincing).

Despite idiotic explanations of his behaviour like his 'jacket getting caught in the doors of the police van when they were slammed shut by a careless policeman', the defendant was found guilty and fined. He claimed to have been outraged by the speed of the police vehicle through the city centre and said he was assaulted when he protested about that. Hence the two complaints against police.

I introduced myself to this young gentleman at the end of the court proceedings, but it was not the ideal time to discuss his grievances against the police so I arranged to meet him later at his home address. 'Play for time' was the only sensible approach here.

A week after the court hearing we met again at his lodgings. He was just as incensed as ever about the speed of the police van through the city centre and the 'rough treatment' he got at the police station. On top of that he now had a conviction for assault on police and breach of the peace. In the time-honoured way I encouraged him to tell me his whole story from the start but it was not going to be easy to take the steam out of this one. He was convinced he was in the right and nothing was going to alter that. I did not bother myself arguing with him but was equally determined that we were not starting a full investigation into nonsense of this sort. His hour of my time was now up, and I said I would call on him again. We parted on good terms.

A couple of weeks later I called again on our hero at his lodgings. This time I was accompanied by a colleague and naturally he had to be regaled with the whole sorry tale from the beginning. Including time at the court hearing, I had already spent many hours listening to all this stuff. While our aggrieved party was in full flight, I took a statement form from my pocket and started to write. To fill a dozen lines or so, I outlined the nature of the complaints and included a reference to the court hearing, then finished it off with a sentence to the effect that there was no need to pursue the complaints any further.

Our hero was so occupied with his tale to my colleague that he hardly seemed to notice me writing. I slid the completed statement form across the table to him and said, 'Right, John, just give us a signature on that and we'll sort it out from here.' He signed without reading it, and I gave my colleague the nudge to indicate that it was time to be off. That was the end of it as far as I was concerned, and nothing more was heard from this man.

Some time after I went to the Complaints Department we got a new chief constable whose surname happened to be the same as mine (but no relation whatsoever). Early press reports about the new man's appointment gave prominence to his pronouncements about wanting to be approachable wherever he happened to be. That seemed to stick in people's minds, although generally members of the public did not appear to know what he looked like.

For me, the first of several instances of mistaken identity occurred in Carlisle about twenty miles from my base, when an elderly lady answered my knock on her front door and immediately replied to my usual form of introduction ('Good morning, madam, my name's Sharpe and I've come from police headquarters') by inviting me to 'Come in, Leslie'. She was only the first of a surprising number of complainants against police who seemed to think it quite natural that the chief constable should come and see them personally about it. This confusion could have advantages and disadvantages – without any subterfuge on my part, I hasten to say.

On one occasion this mistaken identity thing got rather embarrassing. It was a Tuesday morning and I was in my office at police headquarters when the girl at the reception desk rang me to say she had a caller who was 'giving her a bit of bother.' He was insisting on seeing the chief constable about some kind of grievance and she was getting concerned about him. Could I help her? It was not an infrequent occurrence. As usual, I told her to ask the caller to wait and an Inspector Sharpe would be down to see him as soon as possible.

Ten minutes later I found the caller was a middle-aged man who had apparently been involved in a serious road accident about 30 years earlier that had left him disabled due to a head injury. He had been harbouring a grievance all these years about the way he thought the police had handled the accident inquiry and had now decided that our new chief was the man to put things right for him.

The poor man had come about 30 miles by bus for this meeting and he had a lot to say. He jumped to the conclusion that I was the chief, and I did not put him right on that in the belief that at least he might feel better and go away after he had got it all off his chest. About half an hour later I was able to ease him out of the front door of police headquarters and point him back towards his bus home.

I hoped I had seen the last of the unfortunate gentleman but regrettably he turned up again at the same time on Tuesday the following week. By this time it was too late to tell him I was not the chief constable so I just had to let him go on thinking what he wanted. I am afraid he repeated his 30-mile bus trips several more times before they eventually petered out. His judgment was badly impaired, whether that was attributable to the accident all those years ago or not, and there was nothing that I or the chief constable could have done to help him.

Two respectable young men, brothers in fact, became so exasperated with trouble among young people on the Carlisle estate where they lived that one night they took it upon themselves to confront a group of their tormentors. Fearing possible reprisals, one of the brothers wore a balaclava helmet to disguise his identity, but they did take what they regarded as the precaution of getting someone to call the police.

By the time two policemen arrived on the scene in a van, the troublesome young people had disappeared and the two brothers ended up being arrested! They were taken to the police station and detained overnight, and in fact it was not until halfway through the next day that they got back home. When the thing came before the magistrates there were allegations of police heavy-handedness, but a bind-over order was imposed.

The two men had never been in trouble before, and they had quite a grievance against the police over their arrest and the length of time they were kept in custody. I must say I was inclined to sympathise with them, but the fact remained that a court had made its decision after taking account of all the circumstances, so the chances of these two lads achieving any sort of redress through the police complaints procedure were slim, to say the least.

However, complaints had been recorded, and I made arrangements to see them at the home of one of them. Immediately on entering the neat terrace house I noticed I was being received with a remarkable degree of courtesy, indeed deference. My hat and coat were taken and hung up, a tray with coffee and biscuits appeared, the television went off and I was being addressed as 'Sir'. The two young men were accompanied by their mother, a well-dressed middle-aged lady who took an occasional discreet part in the discussion. As I was leaving about an hour later, the lady asked for further confirmation of my identity and remarked that she had taken the day off work specially to meet the chief constable! Oh, dear.

As regards the actual complaint of oppressive conduct by the police, these were decent people whose feelings about what had happened to them that night were quite clear, but there was no getting round the court decision against them. However long it took, I really needed a not pursued result here but this initial meeting was not the time to produce statement forms. Before leaving the house, I suggested they might care to think about discussing the matter with the solicitor who had represented them in court.

I saw the two young men again a week or two later. They seemed rather calmer now. I asked if they had managed to see their solicitor, and they said they had. I wondered if they would mind telling me what he had said about the complaint against police. The elder brother replied, 'He said it was a waste of time complaining.' After a pause he added, 'But you knew he would say that, didn't you?' I looked surprised at that remark and asked how I could possibly have known what their solicitor would say. Anyway, I got my two short not pursued statements signed not long afterwards. There was really no other practical end to this one.

From one or two comments I have made it may be

thought that there was some force in the family solicitor's pragmatic assertion about the value of complaining against the police, although his view of the system may well have been coloured by years of listening to people with criminal convictions who were never going to have anything good to say about the police. Where a complaint seemed genuine, you still had to bear in mind the weight of evidence needed to bring it to a clear-cut conclusion; but even where that level of evidence was lacking, the police force may still have its own ways and means of dealing with something that had apparently gone wrong.

On the other hand, it would not have been right to make complaining an easy option or the whole thing would soon have got out of hand and the police function itself would have become impossible. I did not think there was a simple answer to this, whatever the liberals among us might say. *Quis custodiet ipsos custodes?* Who will watch the watchmen themselves? was no doubt a problem even before the old Roman thought of it and would continue to be a problem for a long time yet, whatever investigative procedures and independent elements were introduced.

Fundamentally, I suppose it would be best for society to keep police powers to the minimum and for the police force to try and ensure that those of its members in close contact with the public are as mature as possible. Perhaps in recent years these ideals had been somewhat eroded.

I think it is on that note that I should begin to wind up these reminiscences of life in the police force. It was now late 1991, and I would soon complete 30 years' pensionable service if I included a year from a previous job that counted for pension purposes. Thirty years' service gave entitlement to a full pension.

I did not think there was much more to learn about this Complaints and Discipline business, and in any case I wanted a new challenge that was unlikely to be achievable within the police. As I looked about me, I had reason to think the police service itself might be approaching the end of one of its better spells in a material sense, although the familiar management problem of complacency was more apparent than ever.

Three decades had passed. I recalled the remarkable characters who had crossed my path – from the 'Christopher Lee/Dracula lookalike' chief constable to fiery super Len of the complaints department and the temperamental German mechanic; the magistrates' clerk with the 'gibbet in the back yard' and the lady court usher with the alluring welcome to her otherwise gloomy domain; the kindly old horse-and-cart-era superintendent urging restraint amid the horror of a police shooting and the jovial sergeant who gave me twenty minutes to lock up a murderous young knifeman on the run.

In a class of his own was 'JJ', flamboyant constable of near-legendary status in the areas of violence and philandering whose expletive-ridden clash with an assertive ambulanceman at the scene of a road accident led to a union-backed complaint which fell to my lot to sort out. Even worse, irrepressible egotist 'JJ' was once seen fighting with another uniformed officer of the law on the road by Ullswater, which at the time was the scene of spectacular activity attracting huge crowds. The hot-headed pair were distracted from their traffic control duties by erotic fantasies about Donald Campbell's glamorous young wife as her speed-ace husband was busy shattering world records and the peace of the valley with his jet-powered hydroplane *Bluebird*.

But enough of the ruminating. Leaving the job after all this time was going to be a problem. To practise the final step, I got myself a piece of paper and pencilled my resignation on it. Eventually I steeled myself to have it typed and signed it. Once I had made the decision, I felt rather more comfortable with what I was doing.

We had a new chief constable by this time. He invited me up to his office for an informal chat and presentation of the usual certificate of service. 'Have you any grievance?' he wondered. No, nothing as negative as that: I was sure I had done a loyal and conscientious job and thought I had the respect of colleagues far and wide.

'What has gone wrong with the police?' he mused. Well, for me the police was at least as good as any other public service, and there was nothing wrong that could not be put right. But surely it was time to take stock. Maybe our relatively favoured financial position in recent years had allowed us to pursue vague notions of better organisational efficiency through modern technology and specialised departments at the expense of public contact at street level. We were losing touch with the people who mattered and they were losing sight of us, while costs were mounting and the press were criticising us more than they used to.

Patient to a fault, the chief did not interrupt as I pressed on with my response to his question. Perhaps policing should be projected primarily as a conspicuous activity in a smart uniform as a clear statement of intent, not just another emergency service rushing about after the event or a technical challenge behind the scenes. Were we getting our priorities wrong in the search for the 'way forward' – a fashionable expression in the job at the time? Without being too cynical, were we tiring of the often boring and messy old business of uniformed patrol – which our paymasters the public still said they wanted to see – in a quest for fresh opportunities that were more easily measurable statistically or simply more exciting? I wished him luck.

ABOUT THE AUTHOR

John Sharpe studied Classics at Durham University and followed National Service in the Army with a working life in the police. A native of Cumbria, he has lived in the county's Eden Valley since the 1960s. His writing speciality is the unsung hero – or villain! The Eden Valley is a rich mine of worthy material.